The Power of Asking
Copyright © 2026 by Inspire Me Enterprises, LLC

All Rights Reserved. Printed in the United States of America.

No part of this book may be used or reproduced in any manner
whatsoever without written permission except in the case of brief
quotations embodied in critical articles and reviews.

ISBN: 978-0615928531

Table of Contents

Praise for The Power of Asking

"If you're looking for a powerful book that will inspire you and convince you no dream is impossible, then read this delightful book."

Jack Canfield
Co-author of Chicken Soup for the Soul® and the Success Principles

"When we shine our light and love as brightly as we possibly can, we give permission for every other human being to do the same thing. *The Power of Asking* shows us that we are all full of the same stuff, and each of us can live an inspirational life!"

Kristine Carlson
Don't Sweat the Small Stuff for Women

"In *The Power of Asking*, Bardi Toto shows how using transformational thinking will allow anybody to step into their greatness and lead extraordinary lives. Through their wisdom and willingness to ask the proper questions, people will touch and inspire countless lives. This book is a must read!"

Les Brown
Top Motivational Speaker, Speech Coach, and Best-Selling Author

"A book every person must read, *The Power of Asking*, is the answer that will awaken the inner self and transform your life forever with transformational thinking."

"The Los Angeles Times"

"Character consists of what you do on the third and fourth try."
- James A. Michener

"Persistence is the desire to have an impact on the world and the determination to act on that desire. While children are born with a motivation to explore and learn, persistence helps them accomplish their goals."

So what happened to us when we became adults? What happened to our persistence?

In *The Power of Asking*, Bardi Toto shares how to get back that persistence to achieve every goal, dream, and desire that you have, so you can make a difference in the world.

People Who Have Used The Power of Asking

"The only 2 reasons people are afraid to ask others for help is either low self-worth or inaccurate beliefs. Low self-worth says, 'If they say no, it means I am not worthy.' This is just an illusion, not a fact. You are more than worthy! Beliefs on the other hand say, 'If you want something done, do it yourself.' This is another mental oversight that is not based in truth, but based on what many have learned when they were children. In either case, learn to get over whatever is holding you back from asking and go for your goals and dreams with total passion, confidence, and certainty, and people will gladly help you!"

John Assaraf

The Secret, Top Motivational Speaker, New York Times Best-Selling Author

"I was going through a difficult time, and I asked myself, 'How am I going to turn this around?' I found myself asking the question, 'What are my gifts, and how can I give more value to the world?' That is when the power of asking changed my whole life."

Kim Coles

Foreword by Michael Bernard Beckwith

Asking empowering questions ignites both the individual and collective evolutionary process. I call questioning an art form because it is a fluid and creative means for opening a treasure trove of self-understanding and insight. When we are willing to ask questions about the meaning and purpose of existence, we are in effect challenging our present paradigms, our preconceived notions, our precious beliefs and concepts. All of this can cause us to feel that we are standing on shaky ground which is why asking questions is the work of a courageous individual.

It could be said that our life direction is informed by the questions we ask. When we ask meaningful questions, the universe responds with meaningful answers. Something fresh emerges, and we see a way out of what at first appeared to be no way. Challenges are redefined and reframed. No matter how technology advances, it cannot outstrip the power that lies within a question.

When our questions are asked from a deeper place within us, they have substance. After all, it was when Einstein saw the sun glittering off flowers that he asked himself if it were possible that he could travel on that very same beam of light. Socrates wrote no papers, and he was a self-described "ignorant man." And yet the Socratic methods display his most potent process: the power of asking the right questions.

In *The Power of Asking*, Bardi Toto has done just that: asked the right questions about questioning, which has led to the wisdom that the answers lie within the questions themselves.

Michael Bernard Beckwith

This book is dedicated to my children, Matthew and Jacob, whom I love beyond words, to my father Richard for always believing in me and being there for me NO MATTER WHAT - even though you have passed over, you are still with me. Also, to everyone who is willing to dream big dreams and has the courage and commitment to ask and take action.

Acknowledgements

Bishop T.D. Jakes – Your work and words has made a huge impact on my life. On January 19, 2014, in a sermon at The Potter's House on Transformation of the Mind, you said, "Don't shape yourself around your thoughts and what has happened in your past; what goes on in your head, goes on in your life; and you can't live it on the outside, if you don't have it in the inside." Thank you for reminding me that I can even further the transformation of my mind.

Michael Bernard Beckwith - Your work and words has made a huge impact on my life. On December 20, 2009, in a sermon you said, "Have Courage to believe what your mind thinks is impossible." Thank you for helping me get out of my head and change my thinking.

To Les Brown, Oprah, Pat Smith, Emmitt Smith and Robin Roberts - Thank you for inspiring me with your story of how the power of asking impacted you on overcoming your obstacles. When you ask and take action, your personal and business life will never be the same. Terry Ilous, thank you for your encouragement and belief in me.

Collin Tipping – Thank you for showing me how to forgive through Radical Forgiveness, the most amazing book and process on forgiving in the world. Anita Rehker, for your encouragement, believing in me, and all your help. Dad- May you rest in peace for always telling me I could do anything I put my mind to, being there no matter what, and encouraging and loving me unconditionally. You showed me how to ask, be persistent, and to go out and do it anyway-even if I'm scared.

To My Clients-Thank you for being part of my life and allowing me to be part of your goals and dreams. Most importantly, thank you to my children Matthew and Jacob, for standing by my side and supporting me in your own ways; you are the best, and I am so blessed to have you. I love you more than anything in the world. Jacob you created the title *The Power of Asking* from my heart. You are going to do big things in this world to serve our country.

Go Out on a Limb,

That is Where the Fruit Is

"Do one thing every day that scares you." —*Eleanor Roosevelt*

I've studied successful people for many years, and although the diversity you find among them is astounding, I have found that they are alike in one way: how they think and a tiny secret they all use, discussed in this book. This is one thing that separates successful people from unsuccessful ones. Here is the good news, how successful people think can be learned, and you can model the action they take.

Good thinking and the power of asking can do many things for you: generate revenue, solve problems, and create opportunities. It can take you to a whole new level - personally and professionally. It can change your life. I know the title of the book is *The Power of Asking*, and you are probably sitting here asking yourself, what does thinking have to do with the power of asking? Let me say this—a lot. When you have that successful good thinking, it will empower you to move big mountains in your life on a personal and business level. It will give you the power to ask.

Limited thinking will keep you in bondage by creating low self-esteem, lack of self-confidence, depression, and anxiety; it will lead you down a road of frustration and to living a life of mediocrity which God did not intend for you. Although I had a father who told me I could do anything I put my mind to and always believed in me, I had other family members who told me the opposite. Unfortunately, sometime the negative words outweigh the positive. If you heard all the time as a child that you will never go to college and won't amount to anything, there is a good chance you may grow up believing that. You can go one of two ways; you can become very successful and surround yourself with positive people or believe what those "naysayers" said and act it out. We hear poison from other individuals who are jealous or envious; however, some of those people we look up to, and end up believing them. If we go into adult hood and end up in negative relationships like the ones we have not healed from in childhood, it can trigger us back to the past, and we tend to react, self-sabotaging our own success and self-worth. I will be the first to admit, I have been guilty of falling prey to that. Remember, if you have experienced this, they were lies out of someone else's mouth, and that does not have to be your mainframe for being your destiny.

I took the positive road, even though I experienced a lot of negativity in my childhood from family members around me; however, it has not been easy. The past few years I have gone through some personal family challenges, and I fought some serious stinking thinking in my head from my past and the negative family that still lingers. Even though the past few years have been challenging, I accomplished some amazing accolades. People know me all over the world for being one of the top branding and social media experts on and offline; however, I am also a bestselling author. The book *Thinking Upside Down Living Rightside Up*: The Way You Think Is How You Live became a best seller on Amazon in less than two hours in the top 3 categories. The forward was written by Michael Bernard Beckwith from the movie The Secret, and it has been endorsed by Jack Canfield, Les Brown, Marie Diamond, Greg S. Reid, and Kristine Carlson just to name a few.

I have been on talk shows, featured in Forbes, on ABC, CBS, NBC radio, written up in business magazines, had VIP treatment at Oprah's Life class, was the social media strategist behind helping with Hurricane Sandy, and the list goes on and on. I am not saying this to impress you, but to impress upon you how changing your thinking will change your life which is my biggest secret revealed in this book the *Power of Asking for Women*. Due to our upbringing and society, what we are told "we should be", others' opinions, and the media, we get caught up in the negativity and obtain a mediocre lifestyle of limited thinking. The 98% believe asking is a form of weakness. On December 20, 2009, in a sermon at Agape, Michael Bernard Beckwith said, "Have courage to believe what your mind thinks is impossible."

Now That's the Life I Want!

"Promise yourself to be strong—that nothing can disturb your peace of mind. Look at the sunny side of everything and make your optimist come true. Think only of the best, work for only the best, and expect only the best. Forget the mistakes of the past and press on to the greater achievements of the future. Give so much time to the improvement of yourself that you have no time to criticize others. Live in the faith that the whole world is on your side so long as you are true to the best that is in you!" **-Christian D. Larson - 1912**

WHY CHANGING YOUR THINKING WILL CHANGE YOUR LIFE?

1. Changed Thinking Is Magical

A change in thinking doesn't happen on its own and somehow appear out of thin air. Good ideas rarely go out and find someone. If you want to find a good idea, you must search for it. For example, I had an idea for a tool everyone needs and must have for an Iphone or smartphone, and now I have the rights to it. It will help millions. I found a solution to a problem. If you want to become an excellent thinker, you need to work at it - and once you become a better thinker, the good ideas keep coming. You can apply this in your personal life as well as your business.

One of the biggest problems among couples is communication. We try and read each other's minds which will lead you down a road of frustration and heartache. I say this from experience; I have been accused of things I was not even thinking and doing. One of my favorite quotes is, "One who tries to read another's mind will be lost."

2. Changed Thinking - YOU CAN DO IT

Albert Einstein, one of the best thinkers who ever lived said, "Thinking is hard work; that's why so few do it." Because thinking is so difficult, you want to use anything you can to help you improve the process. This is why I read positive books and surround myself with people who are good for me. I suggest getting rid of the toxic people in your life or use detachment. Know somebody else's anger is not about you, so do not take it personally. "Hurt people hurt people," and usually with words; they are controlling, manipulative, and demeaning. Changed thinking isn't easy, so get rid of the people who do not support you or your vision in life.

Whatever you do, do not listen to those who may call you a dreamer, make fun of your ideas, or drop comments like "that isn't going to work," "that isn't new," and "someone probably has already done it." You get the picture. That is the 98% telling you that; depending how you were raised, if you are easily triggered, they will suck you into their mediocre lifestyle and negative vortex. Know these people are sick from their own poison they are putting on you, and you do not need to partake in it.

3. Changed Thinking Is Worth the Investment

Napoleon Hill observed, "More gold has been mined from the thoughts of man than has ever been taken from the earth." When you take time to learn how to change your thinking and become a better thinker, you are investing in yourself. Stock markets go south; real estate investments can go sour. But a human mind with the ability to think well is like a diamond mine that never runs out. It's priceless.

In the past, I would hear people's excuses why they couldn't spend money on social media, branding, mentoring, and products among other things. This happened when I was going through my personal challenges and was experiencing "analysis paralysis" and stuck in excuses because of the people I was surrounded by. If people are giving you excuses in your business and personal life, you need to look where in your life you may be making excuses because this will be a full on reflection of what you will get back. Now, I live a life of freedom, not excuses.

 What people don't realize is they are investing in themselves and learning from someone who has been there and done it. Social proof is everything! So when your thinking has gone south, you need to retrain your brain and listen to positive things daily, whether it is reading a book that empowers and inspires you, listening to a CD, or getting on a motivational call. I suggest getting a mentor. I am a mentor to many and have helped thousands succeed, but I also have a mentor, actually a couple.

GETTING OUT OF YOUR OWN WAY

"Fear knocked on the door, faith opened it, and there was no one there."

-Napolean Hill

POWER OF ASKING GEM: FEAR IS BASED ON WHAT WE BELIEVE MIGHT HAPPEN

Fear is not dependent upon an actual happening. You may find you have a fear of poverty. This means you fear, or have an apprehension of, being poor. You are not poor, but you dread that state. Now, if you were in fact poor - totally penniless and at the mercy of charity - you would not fear poverty. Experiencing the state of poverty, you might dislike it, loathe it, or be frustrated by it, BUT YOU WOULD NOT FEAR IT. So it is with all fears. FEAR EXISTS ONLY IN THE UNKNOWN.

Everyone has fears. Every leader, great or small, has had fears at some point in their lives. So the question is not whether or not you have them, but rather, what you do with them, and what you let them do to you. It is a question of, "Who's in Control?" To let fear take over is to let all your energy and personal power pour into that fear. It will become so large that nothing else seems to exist; your world will revolve around fear.

Have you not known someone whose every decision was based on fear? I was there once. An older lady hesitates to make decisions. "I've got to be sure" is her inevitable comment. Needless to say, she does not make decisions; her life just happens. That is fear in almost total control. On the other hand, you can choose to be the one in charge. Faced with a fear, you can decide to continue on, to march ahead even though the worse may happen, and to try even though you may fail. This is what a leader must do. This is the meaning of being a leader. When you do this, you will have the power to ask for what you want in every area of your life and your life will drastically change. You will have unusual success in every area of your life.

In all things, to think is to create. This law is valid in regard to fear as it is in any other area of your life. If you think about fear and what might happen, then that is exactly what will happen. How could it be any other way? Those pictures and thoughts you hold in your mind most of the time will materialize. You will attract what you fear most.

The law works in two ways - for what we desire and for what we dread - or it is not the law. If this were not so, then you would have no choice. You would have no control. There would be no freedom. Liberty could not exist. Through these, we get to experience the thrill of joy and success. We have the opportunity to grow, provided we realize they are experiences and not the final act. Fear is an experience, not a fact.

If you look at the list for business and ask yourself why you have not done those things on your list, the underlying cause will be FEAR.

FEAR stands for False Evidence Appearing Real; fear is one of the most prevalent illusory perceptions in today's world. We see it every day in the media. We see its subtle forms, such as anxiety, stress, nervousness and restlessness. It's based on the illusory belief that someone or something outside ourselves can harm us or destroy our peace of mind. This is only true if we believe we are separate from God and Creation. Once we remove the belief in separation, there is no fear. Seeing that this is an illusion, we can move right through the fear to the reality on the other side.

We must stay fully present with fear -- notice everything about it -- it's color, texture, bodily sensation, how it arises, how it dissolves, what thoughts it generates, what actions we take, how we try to deny it, etc. Avoiding is the fear itself; only awareness dispels it.

Instead of fear, let's look at HOPE and doing our BEST in business and in our personal life. This will help you to master the process of good thinking. Changing my thinking changed my life overnight giving the power of asking.

Helping others

Open doors of opportunity

Pursue

Enthusiasm (Doing it with)

Believe in Yourself

Excellence. Strive for

Serve Others

Take Care of Today

POWER OF ASKING EXERCISE: Write down 10 things you would do if you only had 48 hours. 5 in your business and 5 in your personal life. Now, start with your business and just DO IT as Nike says. Tomorrow is not promised.

STORIES ABOUT THE POWER OF ASKING

Just Be Willing to Ask.

Anonymous

I grew up in a modest Jewish Family. My parents did the best they could with what they had .My mom used to compare me to my "successful " relatives telling me, "Why can't you be more like your cousin or uncle, you're going to be a looser just like your dad" Because of that, I had very low self-esteem and was afraid to ask the right questions or pursue the things I wanted.

The fear of failure and rejection often held me back and left me feeling unworthy. Eventually, I asked myself, "What is holding you back? Why are others successful, and you are not? What is it you fear, and what is this fear costing you?" I imagined all the things that would come into my life if I was just willing to ask. So, I changed the way I approached a situation in order to live a more balanced and successful life. I learned to ask questions, to ask for advice, and to not take no for an answer. Once I altered my mindset, good things began to enter my life.

Ask for What You Want, Be Careful Because You Just Might Get It!

Rich

When I was in my twenties, a high school friend had gone to work on a cruise ship. He was part of the cruise staff and got to travel around the world. When he returned from one of his 6 months at sea gigs, I asked him how difficult it was to get a job like his. He said the competition could be fierce, but if you have a talent that is needed onboard, your chances would improve vastly.

He knew I had been a DJ in a nightclub and told me to contact "Don" who hired the entertainment staff for multiple cruise lines. I was working as a photographer for my dad's ad business at the time and figured, "Why not?"   I had zero expectations. I had always wanted to travel (and get paid for it), and this would be a great way to do it! The interview went pretty well, and I went home and forgot about the whole thing!

A day later, Don called and said, "I've got a six-month cruise in the Eastern Caribbean, and you leave in one week. Can you do it?" I was shocked! My dream job, but can I accept it? My dad was depending on me for his photography and helping around the office. What should I do? I told Don I needed a day to discuss it with my dad. I had not anticipated actually getting the job!

I had a sit down with dad and told him about the job. He was surprised I hadn't mentioned to him I had been considering it. He said that if I were to leave, it would put a damper on his business. I thought long and hard and the next day, I called Don and said, "I have to turn down your offer, my dad needs me." Don said, "I am sorry to hear this; I won't be contacting you again." My heart sank, and I put my head down on my desk and wept. How could I have let it happen this way? My dream job, and I had not prepared my dad for the possibility of me leaving. Now the ship has sailed, and I would never have my chance!

I said to my dad that if the opportunity should come up in the future that I would be going. I never gave up hope that maybe someday I would get another chance. Low and behold, a month later, Don calls! He says he has 6 months with the Holland America Line in the Western Caribbean! "Can you do it?" he asked. "YES, I can!" I said! I told my dad I was leaving in one week! I went to LA to get my tuxedo and uniforms fitted, and the next week I was onboarding the MS Nieuw Amsterdam sailing to Cozumel, Jamaica, and the Cayman Islands!

What an amazing experience to have! 25 years old and I am a DJ in the Pear Tree lounge and experiencing life away from everyone I knew for the first time. It was scary, and what made it more challenging was that it was Thanksgiving, Christmas, New Year's and multiple family birthdays. I found some friends and managed to have a good time exploring.

In addition to working at night as a DJ, I was also cruise staff which meant I worked odd hours and never had a day off. It can wear you out if you don't look after yourself. One thing that I learned and that has always stuck with me since is that we were required to make eye contact and say "hello" to every passenger. We were a "friendly ship"! To this day, I say "hello" to almost everyone and make a point to make eye contact. It makes some people nervous, but it is really nice to show kindness to others as a habit.

After a few months at sea, I got pretty burned out. Working every day and most of the time working on my own in the DJ booth could get pretty lonely. I decided to ask for a shorter contract. Don was not happy and dragged his feet to the point where I was ready to walk. After almost a month, I gave him the ultimatum. "Get me off, or I walk."

I finally got word that a replacement was coming, and 3 and a half months after I started, I was back home. It wasn't so bad, but I realized that being a DJ and working on a cruise ship was not for me. I decided then and there to redouble my efforts with my sports photography. That was, and continues to be, my passion!

I was back working with my Dad and waiting tables at night and getting the occasional sports gigs. Eventually I quit my waiter job and focused more on my photography. It has been thirty years since I started my business, and I am still going!

Here is what I learned.
1. Speak your dreams aloud and someone who can help might hear you.
2. If you want something, ask for it.
3. Be careful what you ask for.
4. If you get it, don't be afraid to admit if you are not happy. You aren't doing anyone any favors by staying in a job you don't like.
5. Sometimes doing something you don't like pushes you in the direction of what you do like!
6. Look for the lessons.
7. Believe in yourself and your abilities.
8. Be grateful for every opportunity.

No regrets for following my dreams- ever. I would rather be poor doing what I love than making lots of money and being unhappy. Do what you love, and the money will hopefully come eventually, and if it doesn't, at least you're doing something that makes you happy!

Oprah says, "You get in life what you have the courage to ask for." I'm a
believer!

Rich has been a photographer since he was a small boy. Growing up in
Huntington Beach, his father would let him take pictures with his Kodak
Duaflex box camera. He was fascinated! By the age of 10, Rich had already
developed his first roll of film and made a contact sheet.

Rich's interest in photography blossomed in high school. He was the photo
editor of Mission Viejo High School's 'Quill and Scroll Award' winning
"Diablo Dispatch". Rich became focused on sports photography and after high
school, he was a stringer for the Saddleback Valley News - covering football,
baseball, and basketball. He also worked for his father's advertising business
doing all the product photography.

In 1984, the Olympic Road Cycling Race was held in Mission Viejo. Rich was
soon a cycling enthusiast and after getting a racing bike, he wanted to shoot
cycling events. At the same time, he also became interested in triathlon. Over
the next 30 years, Rich pursued his dreams and photographed: The Coors
Classic Cycling Race, Tour DuPont, Ironman Triathlon World Championships
in Kona, Hawaii, the 1996 Olympics in Atlanta, and was the official
photographer for the XTERRA Off-road Triathlon Series and the ITU World
Cup Triathlon Series. Rich is currently the official photographer for the LA
Marathon and works extensively with USA Triathlon and the Challenged
Athletes Foundation.

His images have appeared in: People, Outside, Runner's World, Triathlete,
Reader's Digest, Men's Journal, and countless books.

Upon moving to Vista, Rich quickly discovered the magic of Oceanside -
particularly at sunset. "The beach here is pure magic. I am constantly
astounded on the diversity I find. I love the pelicans, the pier and the harbor.
Low tide at sunset in Oceanside is like a symphony. Being here is a great way
to end my day and celebrate another day on earth. It is a sort of meditation for
me. It brings me joy."

Rich connected with Oprah Winfrey via twitter when he tweeted a photo of a
woman with her baby at sunset. They became friends, and he has met her in
person 6 times. Oprah purchased one of Rich's photos for her home in Maui.

Asking Creates Success.

Anonymous

Bardi and I have been friends for quite some time, and heavily connected via the social media world.

I love Bardi's mission with *The Power of Asking* and empowering people to ask because it can change your life, as it has mine.

Bardi asked me to tell my story about the first time I asked and *The Power of Asking*. It really made me think about when I did first ask, and how far that has gotten me.

The first time I truly asked for an opportunity was when I was transitioning from the corporate design world in NYC to the entertainment and film industry. I asked my uncle who's a top executive in the film industry for a chance to learn that side of the business. And trust me it didn't happen that easily. I had to get out of my own comfort zone and challenge myself to ask for more and push for the job I wanted to be a part of and keep asking and pursuing till I received it. From asking, I was able to not only interview, but end up being hired and working for the amazing director Oliver Stone and incredible costume designer Ellen Mirojnick on "Wall Street:Money Never Sleeps". I learned from both of these incredible people and their teams who are now still my mentors in this business today.

Even now as my own business owner and celebrity stylist, I have to continually ask. I have to ask for jobs, I have to ask for clients to trust my vision, I have to ask for opportunities for new projects, I have to ask, period. As my own business, I go through many of my own struggles and successes, and the reason I use struggles is because nothing you ever do is a failure. My father, who's an esteemed top executive himself, always tells me and taught me that you never fail; everything is a learning curve. He has always taught me not to quit, and that sticks within me.

Asking has opened so many doors and opportunities for me. From asking, I've seen progress in my own business and building within myself.
However, there's a fine line from asking too much. You have to be well equipped within yourself. Passionate, hardworking, driven, great attitude,

whatever it may be for you. Invest in yourself. Think of yourself as an investment. You have to be willing to put in the hard work.

My journey began with asking. I have to say I have learned more about myself from this, and I have learned that you have to get uncomfortable to get comfortable again and to succeed and to take yourself to the next level.

I will leave you with this, I always say and teach my clients & believe in this as well, "Confidence is your best accessory".
Be confident within yourself and your dreams!
You are a diamond, Doll. You're fabulous; you're worth it!

Fears Emotions - Positive or Negative

What is fear's purpose? How do you handle it? While I am working in my pest control business, I meet people almost on a daily basis who are influenced by negative fear thoughts regarding pests invading their premises. A good size spider, rat, or unexpected insect can set someone off pretty quickly and literally immobilize them. It consumes their thoughts to the point where they have trouble thinking about anything else.

Thinking about why people do this makes me wonder about the purpose of fear emotions. I really started wondering as to how many people really do allow fear, anxiety, worry, etc. to freeze them into inaction in everyday life. They achieve a very negative result, one which I have to think, is not what they really want.

Fear - What is its purpose? Do you let fear immobilize you, or do you act in spite of it-safely, consciously aware of why it is there?

Personally, I look upon fear as a positive emotion. I know that uncontrolled, this emotion can breed many negative results. But when controlled, this emotion can spur you into action like no other I know of. And I think that this is truly the reason for fear. Think of it as your best friend, preparing you for progress. Make friends with the unknown.

We should acknowledge the fear we are experiencing. Allow that it is a positive thing within us that warns us of some impending danger or harm. And then, analyze it to see if it is real or imagined, justified or not. When we recognize its positive intent, it is no longer something to immobilize us, but quite the reverse; we can jump into action to remedy 'why' we are fearful.

I think that it is the inaction bred by over-analyzing, by focusing on the fear, actually dwelling on it, imagining the 'what ifs', that keeps us from taking the actions necessary to move through it. We need to process it, not dwell in it. I'm sure everyone has heard the old expression, 'A coward dies a thousand deaths, a brave person, only one.' We do not want to hold the FEAR thought. That is not what it is there for.

As long as we focus on the positive intent a fearful state represents, rather on the fear itself, we can question ourselves as to what this fear is trying to tell us to do and take the necessary actions to protect ourselves or blast us though this perceived barrier.

All we have to know is, 'What is really going on here?' What do I need to do in order for me to feel better about moving forward, or do I really need to back off from this course? Do I need to take another smaller action (baby step), or do I just need to change my perception about what is going on here?"

Then, move forward in some direction, no matter how small a step it seems. Usually, just taking action and the momentum you gain and feel, will free you from the fearful, concerned, worried feeling you had.

Do you have something bothering you, or something you have been putting off, or dreading? Something you know you must do, but just haven't been able to face up to the task? Break it down until there is something you can move forward with. Take it in baby steps, take action. Do it and then celebrate the victory! Feel your confidence grow!

Your mind can only hold one thought at a time. Make it an action thought that empowers you.

"IF IT IS IMPORTANT TO YOU, YOU WILL FIND A WAY. IF NOT, YOU'LL FIND AN EXCUSE" - unknown

Fear sounds like this: EXCUSES FOR A CLOSED MIND

- I don't have time.

- It costs too much.

- That's not my job.

- I don't have enough help.

- I will do it later.

- I am too young.

- I am too old.

- I am busy.

- I will do it tomorrow.

- I need to ask my spouse.

- My past is too dark.

- I am a single mom or dad.

- That's just not me.

- I don't know anybody.

- I don't like flying.

- It is too far.

- I don't have enough or don't want to waste my gas (poverty mindset).

- We've always done it this way.

- I need to sleep on it.

- Too much trouble to change

- I know others who tried it, and it did not work.

- It isn't in the budget.

- I am too old to change.

- They will laugh at us.

- Has anyone else tried it?

- People won't buy it.

- Get back to reality.

- I am not technical, or I don't know how to use a computer.

- I am computer challenged.

- It's impossible.

POWER OF ASKING ACTION STEP FOR EXCUSES: Financially, where would your life be right now if you had not made excuses this year? Looking at the list above, how many of these excuses did you use? Did you gain anything by making excuses? What did you lose? Was it Time? Money? Companionship? Insecurity? Self-Esteem? Self-Confidence?

*If you hate getting excuses from your kids, then why are you making them? Your children learn by example, and the way you live is how you will lead.

The Results of My Fears

If my worst fears came true, how would they impact me?

How do my fears affect the way I make decisions?

What provokes my fears?

How to stop getting excuses in your business and personal life:

1. Get over your own excuses in your life. Look at yourself and where you are in your life with them. Do you make a lot of excuses?

2. On a scale of 1-10, how do you rate your life in terms of the excuses you use?

3. Stop giving reasons why you are upset with your spouse, or why you were laid off. Stop arguing and defending, or you will stay stuck. These are excuses.

4. Instead of giving reasons why you can't, find a way to propel yourself forward to get results.

5. If you don't get out there, you are going to lose the opportunity helping others and being the success God meant for you to be.

Lies Society and other People instill in us:

1. Don't dream.

2. Don't hope.

3. It probably is not going to work anyway, so why bother, why try?

    This is where we stop advancing because we have been conditioned to settle for less, in business and in our personal life.

The Power of Asking vs. Not Asking at All

I am no different than you. In January 2007, I got married; my husband of only 8 months suffered a brain injury, and he was in a coma and on a ventilator. Suddenly, I found myself taking care of 5 people, not knowing if he was going to return to work. I suffered daily from anxiety, PTSD from his freak accident, and in March 2008, I found one of my mentors in Dallas, Texas at the Intercontinental Hotel. I started my own marketing company 17 years earlier, and it was an overnight success. Parallel to this, I was a nurse by trade. Yes, a nurse. I loved helping others, but couldn't stand the politics, so I took my love of helping others to my marketing company and online. I am thankful God favored me with my talents, or I would have had to get several jobs. This was great, but something was missing. There is a difference between treating your business as a hobby versus a business. My underlying fear which was keeping me in bondage was that I wanted to be everything to everybody. Growing up around several toxic people didn't help. I became an overachiever, people pleaser, but for the wrong reasons and helped the wrong people. I wanted to prove to myself what they said were lies. Now, I know they were.

I left the conference on fire. The one question she asked that struck me to my inner core was the following: if you had 48 hours to live, what would you do? She continued to say watch what rises up in you. My list got big quickly, and then it hit me how I had settled for less in all areas of my life. I suddenly started asking myself 'why not' questions. Why couldn't I be an author? Why couldn't Michael Beckwith write the foreword of my book? Why couldn't I be on TV? Why not? I wanted to write a book, I wanted my book to be a best seller, I wanted my book to be seen by millions, I wanted to do mission work in third world countries, I wanted to be on talk shows, I wanted to be on radio, I wanted to help others find their light and make a mark on the world. I wanted to make my own social media and branding products, I wanted to show people how to use social media vs just selling them information like 98% of the internet does. Guess what? I have done all of this and more. The book took a while because of my former husband's situation, but I accomplished tons of other accolades beyond my imagination.

In 2011, my book *Thinking Upside Down Living Rightside Up* became a number 1 best seller out of the top 3 categories on Amazon, Michael Beckwith did write the foreword of my book, and I got the endorsements I wanted; in 2009 and 2010, I was approached by Shark Tank for my product The Social Media Profit System; 2012 and 2013 included numerous write ups in magazines, radio shows and talk shows, voted #2 out of the top 100 branding experts to follow online and #4 in Social Media, and I have met some amazing individuals of notoriety. In late 2012, I was found on social media by

NBC and asked to cover Hurricane Sandy. What an honor to help millions of people. In February 2013, I went with a group of women to Costa Rica, and we took school supplies into the villages; what a life changing event. This all happened very fast and virally. I will share shortly how I did it. Once again, all of this is not to impress you, but to impress upon you that I am no different than you.

Did I backslide? For the past 2 years my father was terminal with CHF and many other health ailments, and he finally passed May 19, 2013. He would not allow anybody to care for him but me, so I thank God, once again, I work for myself. I still had accolades and amazing things, however my excuses came back because I was mentally exhausted.

As children, we were persistent. If you remember, as a child you did not have a problem bugging your parents for that toy, ice cream cone, or saving money for that bike. We did not give up until we got what we wanted. We had childlike faith, but what happened as we grew up? We heard the negative tapes and lies we were told. Then we became conditioned and domesticated to settle for less. We have gotten into a status quo of a rut where we have forgotten what that sense of urgency and persistence feels like.

Following are examples of how persistence develops in the first three years of life:

- A 6-week-old smiles at her mother. Her mother smiles back and gives her a kiss. The baby smiles again and receives another smile and kiss in return. This baby is learning that she has the power to impact her world and receive a positive, loving response from another person.

- A 9-month-old drops his spoon over the side of his high chair. He laughs at the clatter it makes and is thrilled when his older brother reaches down and returns it to him. He promptly throws it back on the floor as he and his brother laugh at this silly game. This baby is learning that he can make a loud noise, create a fun game, get someone to act on his behalf, and make this special someone laugh.

- An 18-month-old lifts a marker to the wall—he has a huge, wide open space to decorate. After only a few minutes, his mother swoops down and grabs the marker from his hand. She looks angry and talks to him in a stern voice. This toddler is learning that sometimes his goals don't please the people he loves. It is the beginning of learning about appropriate behavior and making wise choices about his actions that will continue as he grows.

- A 2-year-old carefully stacks one block on top of another to make a tower. He experiments with which blocks form the most solid base and considers how best to balance the blocks as the tower gets taller. This toddler is learning what steps are involved in making his goal a reality through careful planning and persistence.

Being Unstoppable in 4 Easy Steps

Never underestimate the power of persistence!

If you persist you really cannot fail. While you may fail many times along the way, you have not truly failed until you accept failure. However, if you are truly persistent, failure is a clear indication you are getting closer to success. How can that be? Because with each failure comes very valuable knowledge-the knowledge of what DOESN'T work which is the basic premise of testing.

Acknowledging failure brings you a step closer to success, and you will never look at it the same way again. Do you have a light in your house? Of course, you do. Do have light in your car? Of course, you do. Do you see them in the street, in the shops, airports, hospitals, restaurants etc? Yes, they are everywhere. Well, the electric light was borne from one man's irresistible persistence to invent what many said was impossible.

It wasn't easy, thousands of times he failed.... thousands!!How many people make it past 3 failures? Most give up after only one. Plenty never even try. But Thomas A. Edison, the creator of the incandescent light, took each of those failures in his stride. With the knowledge of what DOESN'T work, each failure took him a step closer to changing the entire world! If persistence can change the world, imagine what it can do for you.

Persistence can be developed through 4 simple steps.

Pay close attention, these are life skills you should embrace deep within your psyche...practice them whenever you want to rise above your present dilemma...teach them to your children!

The 4 Steps to Developing Persistence:

1. Have a definite goal fueled by a burning desire to achieve it.

2. Have a definite plan and continually work at it.

3. Close your mind against all negativity. Do not think about or be discouraged by the negative comments that may come from family, friends and acquaintances.

4. Form a friendship with one or more people who will encourage you to follow through with your plan and achieve your goals. If you know people of similar mind, then that is fantastic; spend time with them, soak up their positivity. If not, don't worry because you do not necessarily need to forma

personal relationship. Encouragement from the great minds and achievers of our time can be found in books, DVD's and CD's. Persistence is a necessary ingredient in any achievement. Obviously, it must be because if you didn't persist, you would never finish anything. The degree of your persistence is actually proportional to the size of the achievement. It has been a defining characteristic of some of the greatest men and women to ever walk our planet. So how did I do all of this? First, I got rid of my excuses, got my childlike persistence back, and implemented successful thinking. Here is the biggest secret, very small and simple . . . I asked!

I did not just ask, but I built relationships. I asked for what I wanted, but I also asked questions and genuinely wanted to know about the other person. I asked questions about their family, their hobbies, where they went to school. Every person I have ever met on the phone or in person, I have had something in common with. Example: if you are speaking to someone from Houston, Texas, more than likely you have been there, or know someone from there; or perhaps you have been to Texas, want to go there, or have a friend from there. The Power of Asking is not just about asking or asking questions. First, you must get the successful thinking down which is what I have been talking about so far in this book. If you do not have the successful thinking, get rid of the excuses, or the power of asking won't work. I will go over some techniques and strategies regarding the power of asking.

Expectations are Excuses and Breed Resentments

Some of the expectations I have heard over the years are women should be this way, men should be that way, or you may have a mother or father who have always done it a certain way. It doesn't have to be done the way it always has been done. Even opinions can stem from expectations.
The bottom line is that expectations are excuses.

"Our lives are shaped not as much by experience as by our expectations." -
George Bernard Shaw

What are expectations, and why do we have them?

Although this may sound like a simple question, it really has two answers - a conscious answer and a subconscious answer. In either case, though, we can agree that an expectation is what one believes must be furnished or established in order for that person to take action, or for that action to be meaningful or effective. And usually that which is necessary to be furnished or established is something that someone else (person, company, government) must supply.
When we enter into any kind of relationship (work is a relationship), we have expectations of which some are defined, and some are assumed.
Right away, one can see that this has an immediate possibility for problems to arise. The assumptions we make can wreak havoc on our attitudes and subsequently, our beliefs, and as we know, belief is elemental to success.
That being the case, it is important for us to know the motive of our expectations. This becomes especially true, albeit more difficult, for our subconscious (automatic and assumed) expectations. But to better understand our subconscious expectations, it is necessary to first understand our conscious expectations.

Our conscious expectations are what is agreed upon by two parties when they enter into a relationship.

For instance, if you engage in a sales career, the company may say that they will supply everything you need to become a successful agent. The only thing you have to provide is the sales. Subconsciously, you attach certain requirements (expectations) to those things that the company provides. So you expect a "good" product, "professional" marketing materials, and a "competitive" price. Although these expectations are not unreasonable, they are subjective, and that's when the problems arise! What one person thinks is good might be considered bad by someone else. Now, you can see why it's so important that one knows their own personal subconscious expectations.

Conscious or subconscious, our expectations are what we expect others to do, in order for us to be successful.

And therein lays the problem because you are giving others the power to control your destiny. If by having expectations, we are saying that we can't be successful unless someone else supplies those expectations, then you must understand that the following:

It is unreasonable to expect anyone to be as interested in your success as you are.

There are always alternatives! For instance, if the company doesn't provide you with what you consider to be enough leads, then you can also generate them yourself! Keep that power over your destiny in your own hands, even though the alternatives may sometimes be tough and work intensive.

The truth is that your expectations are excuses.

If you do not succeed, you will point to the expectations that others did not fulfill as the reason for your lack of success. But don't take it personal- everybody does it! The reality is that because of our conditioning and programming from our youth, we use expectations to begin the rationalization process for our possible failure-even before we begin the endeavor!

We subconsciously give more attention, initially, to our possibility of failure than to our possibility of success through the formation of our expectations.

We do this unconsciously, but because this is true, we are often not as successful as we are capable of becoming. Knowing this is enough to tip the scales in the other direction.

Examine your expectations for clues to the conditioning and programming that result in lack of success,s and you can change your life.

POWER OF ASKING ACTION STEP: What is a subconscious expectation you currently have that is bugging the heck out of you because you're not getting it? It can be in any kind of relationship: work, family, and romantic.

Change is Inevitable, Suffering is Optional!

"Do one thing everyday that scares you" - Eleanor Roosevelt

Action Rules - Just Get Started!

'Action Rules!' in the Getting Goals Game. It is the number one most important step to achieving your greatness. Having second thoughts? Trouble getting started. Stalled on a plateau? Spinning your wheels trying to get going again? Just get started. Goal setting and planning are necessary, but 'Action Rules' when it comes to getting what you want. Like Nike says, 'Just Do It!'

Taking action, any action, is the important step. As long as you are moving, you can use the momentum to take more action. The saying that you can't steer a parked car is right on. You must get your vehicle moving before you can steer it. You can even change vehicles to get to where you want to go, but you must start movement in the beginning. You can even change the direction, (your destination), but getting started is all important.

No action is too small to start with. In fact, the smaller the better because it is sometimes easier to believe in doing little things, then you can move up incrementally to larger steps when you gain momentum and confidence. Remember the things you get will not make you happy; it is the challenge and the accomplishment of the things that create happiness. Too many people achieve to be happy, rather than happily achieve. The joy is in the journey, not the journey's end.

Start moving towards your dream. Get off that couch, turn off that TV, stop daydreaming about what you would like to be or do, and start with some action that will take you in the direction that you want to go. Maybe you have been able to fulfill most of what you want to do. Is there still something in your life that you have got to do, but are feeling stuck and just haven't been able to get it?? Well, if you still want to try, then this is the place to get unstuck!

'Don't know where to go or what to do?' Decide for now that you do know, pick that thing that keeps coming into your mind, but you brush it away when your self-talk keeps telling you, "I couldn't possibly do that." Do it! You can change your mind later, if need be. Just get rolling! Get started! You can do it! Be courageous! You will find that in starting anything worthwhile, you will feel some reluctance to believe that you can do it. You will sometimes feel the force of inertia. Most of us have felt this. Just remember that many people who have achieved greatness, felt that same emotion at times. They just refused to believe that they couldn't do it and went ahead on faith that it would work out. Move forward.

The reason for doing something is far more important in motivating you than the thing itself, so pump up the urgency by focusing on your outcome and how it will feel when you achieve it, instead of whether you can or cannot do it. Because you can at least get it started! Take the first step into the rest of your life. Just begin! Remember 'ACTION RULES!'

HOW TO ACHIEVE POWERFUL SUCCESSFUL THINKING

Engaging in an ongoing process improves your thinking:

1. Expose Yourself to Good Input:

Successful thinkers always prime the pump of ideas. They always look for things to get the thinking process started because what you put in, always impacts what comes out. Read books, magazines, listen to CDs and spend time with successful good thinkers. When something intrigues you - whether it's someone else's idea or the seed of an idea that you've come up with yourself - keep it in front of you. Put it in writing and keep it somewhere in your favorite thinking place to stimulate your thinking.

2. Expose Yourself Around Powerful Successful Thinking People

Spend time with the right people. These are people who want to grow and learn. It is amazing as I look back on the past 7 years who I chose to surround myself with and whom I attracted. All of them were people

3. Choose to Think Positive Thoughts

To become a positive thinker, you must become intentional about the thinking process. Regularly put yourself in the right place to think, shape, stretch, and land your thoughts. Make it a priority. Remember, thinking is a discipline.

4. Act on Your Good Thoughts

Ideas have e a short shelf life. You must act on them before the expiration date. "I can give you a six-word formula for success: Think things through — then follow through."

5. Allow Your Emotions to Create Another Good Thought

To start the thinking process, you cannot rely on your feelings. If you wait until you feel like doing something, you will likely never accomplish it. The same is true for thinking. You cannot wait until you *feel* like thinking to do it. However, I've found that once you engage in the process of good thinking, you can use your emotions to feed the process and create mental momentum.

Try it yourself. After you go through the disciplined process of thinking and enjoy some success, allow yourself to savor the moment and try riding the mental energy of that success.

6. Repeat the Process

One good thought does not make a good life. The people who have one good thought and try to ride it for an entire career often end up unhappy or destitute. They are the one-hit wonders, the one-book authors, the one-message speakers, and the one-time inventors who spend their life struggling to protect or promote their single idea. Success comes to those who have an entire mountain of gold that they continually mine, not those who find one nugget and try to live on it for fifty years. To become someone who can mine a lot of gold, you need to keep repeating the process of good thinking.

PUTTING YOURSELF IN THE RIGHT PLACE TO THINK

Becoming a good thinker isn't overly complicated. It's a discipline. If you do the six things I have outlined above, you will set yourself up for a lifestyle of successful powerful thinking. But what do you do to come up with specific ideas on a day-to-day basis?

1. Find a Place to Think Your Thoughts

If you go to your designated place to think expecting to generate good thoughts, then eventually you will come up with some. Where is the best place to think? Everybody's different. I believe I often get thoughts because I make it a habit to frequently go to my thinking places. If you want to consistently generate ideas, you need to do the same thing. Find a place where you can think and plan to capture your thoughts on paper so that you don't lose them. When I found a place to think my thoughts, my thoughts found a place in me.

2. Find a Place to Shape Your Thoughts

Rarely, do ideas come fully formed and completely worked out. Most of the time, they need to be shaped until they have substance. Many times a thought that seemed outstanding late at night looks pretty silly in the light of day. Ask questions about your ideas. Fine tune them. One of the best ways to do that is to put your thoughts in writing. As you shape your thoughts, you find out whether an idea has potential. You learn what you have. You also learn something about yourself.

You can shape your thoughts almost anywhere. Just find a place that works for you, where you will be able to write things down, and focus your attention without interruptions. And ask questions about your ideas.

3. Find a Place to Stretch Your Thoughts

If you come upon great thoughts and spend time mentally shaping them, don't think you're done and can stop there. If you do, you will miss some of the most valuable aspects of the thinking process. You miss bringing others in and expanding ideas to their greatest potential.

Earlier in my life, I have to admit, I was often guilty of this error. I wanted to take an idea from seed thought to solution before sharing it with anyone, even the people it would most impact. I did this both at work and at home. But over the years, I have learned that you can go much farther with a team than you can go alone.

I've found a kind of formula that can help you stretch your thoughts. It says:

The Right **Thought** plus the Right **People**

In the Right **Environment** at the Right **Time**

For the Right **Reason** = the Right **Result**

This combination is hard to beat. Like every person, every thought has the potential to become something great. When you find a place to stretch your thoughts, you find that potential.

4. Find a Place to Put Your Thoughts

Any idea that remains only an idea doesn't make a great impact. The real power of an idea comes when it goes from abstraction to application. If you want your thoughts to make an impact, you need to land them with others so that they can someday be implemented. As you plan for the application phase of the thinking process, land your ideas first with the following people:

- **Yourself:** Landing an idea with yourself will give you integrity. People will buy into an idea only after they buy into the leader who communicates it. Before teaching others, ask three questions: *"Do I believe it? Do I live it? Do I believe others should live it?"* If I can answer yes to all three questions, then I have landed it.

- **Key Players**: Let's face it; no idea will fly if the influencers don't embrace it. After all, they are the people who carry thoughts from idea to implementation.

- **Those Most Affected**: Landing thoughts with the people on the firing line will give you great insight. Those closest to changes that occur as a result of a new idea can give you a "reality read." And that's important because sometimes even when you've diligently completed the process of creating a thought, shaping it, and stretching it with other good thinkers, you can still miss the mark.

Finding a Place to Make Your Thoughts Soar

What good is thinking if it has no application in real life? Learning how to master the process of thinking well leads you to productive thinking. If you can develop the discipline of good thinking and turn it into a lifetime habit, then you will be successful and productive all of your life. Once you've created, shaped, stretched, and landed your thoughts, then flying them can be fun and easy.

PORTRAIT OF A POWERFUL SUCCESSFUL THINKER

You often hear someone say that a colleague or friend is a "good thinker," but that phrase means something different to everyone. To one person it may mean having a high IQ, while to another it could mean knowing a bunch of trivia, or being able to figure out whodunit when reading a mystery novel. I believe that good thinking isn't just one thing. It consists of several specific thinking skills. Becoming a good thinker means developing those skills to the best of your ability.

ELEPHANT THINKING

Thinking can benefit any person in any profession. Real estate developer Donald Trump quipped, "You have to think anyway, so why not think big?" Elephant thinking brings wholeness and maturity to a person's thinking. It brings perspective. It's like making the frame of a picture, and in the process, expanding not only what you can see, but what you are able to do.

Spend time with Elephant thinkers, and you will find that they:
Learn Continually

Elephant thinkers are never satisfied with what they already know. They are always visiting new places, reading new books, meeting new people, learning new skills. And because of that practice, they often are able to connect the unconnected. They are lifelong learners. To help me maintain a learner's attitude, I spend a few moments every morning thinking about my learning opportunities for the day. As I review my calendar and to-do lists—knowing whom I will meet that day, what I will read, which meetings I will attend–**I** note where I am most likely to learn something. Then I mentally cue myself to look attentively for something that will improve me in that situation. If you desire to keep learning, I want to encourage you to examine your day and look for opportunities to learn.

Listen Intentionally

An excellent way to broaden your experience is to listen to someone who has expertise in an area where you don't. I search for such opportunities. Listening has taught me a lot more than talk. When you meet with people, it's good to have an agenda, so that you can learn. It's a great way to partner with people who can do things you can't. Elephant thinkers recognize that they don't know lots of things. They frequently ask penetrating questions to enlarge their understanding and thinking. If you want to become a better elephant thinker, then become a good listener.

Look Expansively

Human beings habitually see their own world first. For example, when people arrive at a leadership conference put on by my company, they want to know where they're going to park, whether they will be able to get a good (and comfortable) seat, whether the speaker will be "on," and if the breaks will be spaced right.

Elephant thinkers realize there is a world out there besides their own, and they make an effort to get outside. It's hard to see the picture while inside the frame. To see how others see, you must first find out how they think. Becoming a good listener certainly helps with that. So does getting over your personal agenda and trying to take the other person's perspective.

Live Completely

The truth is that you can spend your life any way you want, but you can spend it only once. Becoming an elephant thinker can help you to live with wholeness and to live a very fulfilling life. People who see the big picture expand their experience because they expand their world. As a result, they accomplish more than narrow-minded people. They experience fewer unwanted surprises, too, because they are more likely to see the many components involved in any given situation: issues, people, relationships, timing, and values. They are also, therefore, usually more tolerant of other people and their thinking.

WHY YOU SHOULD RECEIVE ELEPHANT THINKING

Intuitively, you probably recognize elephant thinking as beneficial. Few people want to be close-minded. No one sets out to be that way. But just in case you're not completely convinced, consider several specific reasons why you should make the effort to become a better big-picture thinker:

1.   Elephant Thinking Allows You to Lead

You can find many "big-picture" elephant thinkers who aren't leaders, but you will find few leaders who are not elephant thinkers. Leaders must be able to do many important things for their people:

> · **See the vision before their people do**. They also see more of it. This allows them to…

- **Size up situations**, taking into account many variables. Leaders who see the big picture discern possibilities as well as problems to form a foundation to build the vision. Once leaders have done that, they can…

- **Sketch a picture of where the team is going**, including any potential challenges or obstacles. The goal of leaders should not be merely to make their people feel good, but to help them be good and accomplish the great. The vision shown accurately, will allow leaders to…

- **Show how the future connects with the past to make the journey more meaningful.** When leaders recognize this need for connection and bridge it, then they can…

- **Seize the moment when the timing is right.** In leadership, when to move is as important as what you do. As Winston Churchill said, "There comes a special movement in
- everyone's life, a moment for which that person was born; when he seizes it, it is his finest hour."

Whether building roads, planning a trip, or moving in leadership, big-picture thinking allows you to enjoy more success. People who are constantly looking at the whole picture have the best chance of succeeding in any endeavor.

2.   Elephant Thinking Keeps You on Target

To get things done, you need focus. However, to get the right things done, you also need to consider the big picture. Only by putting your daily activities in the contest of the big picture will you be able to stay on target. "You've got to think about 'big things' while you're doing small things, so that all the small things go in the right direction." - Michael Beckwith

Elephant Thinking Allows You to see What Others See

One of the most important skills you can develop in human relations is the ability to see things from the other person's point of view. It's one of the keys to working with clients, satisfying customers, maintaining a marriage, rearing children, helping those who are less fortunate, etc. All human interactions are enhanced by the ability to put yourself in another person's shoes. How? Look beyond yourself, your own interest, and your own world. When you work an issue from every possible angle, examine it in the light of another's history, discover the interests and concerns of others, and try to set aside your own agenda, you begin to see what others see. And that is a powerful thing.

3. Elephant Thinking Promotes Teamwork

If you participate in any kind of team activity, then you know how important it is that team members see the whole picture, not just their own part. Anytime a person doesn't know how his work fits with that of his teammates, then the whole team is in trouble. The better the grasp team members have of the big picture, the greater their potential to work together as a team.

4. Big-Picture Thinking Keeps You from Being Caught Up in the Mundane

Let's face it; some aspects of everyday life are absolutely necessary, but thoroughly uninteresting. Elephant thinkers don't let the grind get to them because they don't set sight on the all-important overview. They know that the person who forgets the ultimate is a slave to the immediate.

5. Elephant Thinking Helps You to Chart Unchartered Territory

Have you ever heard the expression, "We'll cross that bridge when we come to it?" That phrase undoubtedly was coined by someone who had trouble seeing the big picture. The world was built by people who "crossed bridges" in their minds long before anyone else did. The only way to break new ground or move into uncharted territory is to look beyond the immediate and see the big picture.

HOW TO ACQUIRE THE WISDOM OF ELEPHANT SIZE THINKING

If you desire to seize new opportunities and open new horizons, then you need to add big-picture thinking to your abilities. To become a good thinker and be able to see the big picture, keep in mind the following suggestions:

1. Don't Strive for Certainty

Elephant thinkers are comfortable with ambiguity. They don't try to force every observation or piece of data into pro-formulated mental cubby holes. They think broadly and can juggle many seemingly contradictory thoughts in their minds. If you want to cultivate the ability to think big-picture, then you must get used to embracing and dealing with complex and diverse ideas.

2. Learn from Every Experience

Elephant thinkers broaden their outlook by striving to learn from every experience. They don't rest on their successes, they learn from them. More importantly, they learn from their failures. They can do that because they remain teachable.

Varied experiences-both positive and negative—help you see the big picture. The greater the variety of experience and success, the more potential you have to learn. If you desire to be a big-picture thinker, then get out there and try a lot of things, take a lot of chances, and take time to learn after every victory or defeat.

3. Gain Insight from a Variety of People

Elephant thinkers learn from their experiences, but they also learn from experiences they don't have. That is, they learn by receiving insight from others—from customers, employees, colleagues, and leaders.

If you desire to broaden your thinking and see more of the big picture, then seek out counsels to help you. But be wise in whom you seek for advice. Gaining insight from a variety of people doesn't mean stopping anyone and everyone in hallways and grocery store lines and asking what they think about a given subject. Be selective. Talk to people who know and care about you, who know their field, and who bring experience deeper and broader than your own.

4. Give Yourself Permission to Expand Your World

If you want to be an elephant thinker, you will have to go against the flow of the world. Society wants to keep people in boxes. Most people are married mentally to the status quo. They want what was, not what can be. They seek safety and simple answers. To think big-picture, you need to give yourself permission to go a different way, to break new ground, to find new worlds to conquer. And when your world does get bigger, you need to celebrate. Never forget that there is more out there in the world than what you've experienced.

Keep learning, keep growing; keep looking at the big picture! If you desire to be a good thinker, that's what you need to do.

Focused Successful Thinking

WHERE SHOULD YOU FOCUS YOUR THINKING?

Be selective, not exhaustive, in your focused thinking. That means dedicating in-depth thinking time to four areas: leadership, creativity, communication, and international networking. Here are some steps you can take:

Identify Your Priorities

First, take into account your priorities-for yourself, your family, and your team. Unfortunately, many people land on priorities based on where they run out of steam. You certainly don't want to do that, nor do you want to let others set your agenda.

There are many ways to determine priorities. If you know yourself well, begin by focusing on your strengths - the things that make the best use of yourself and God-given talents. You might also focus on what brings the highest return and reward. Do what you enjoy most and do best. You could use the 80/20 rule. Give 80 percent of your effort to the top 20 percent most important activities. Another way is to focus on exceptional opportunities that provide a huge return. It comes down to this: *give your attention to the areas that bear fruit.*

Discover Your Gifts

Hire a coach or mentor if you need to do so. Not all people are self-aware and have a good handle on their own skills, gifts, and talents. I have helped hundreds find their talents they have been given and act on them.

I've met many individuals who grew up in a houseful of people who received little encouragement or affirmation, and as a result, seem at a loss for direction. I experienced this, as well as a positive parent, which left me at one time extremely confused. If you have that kind of background, you need to work extra hard to figure out what your goals are. Spend some time reflecting on past successes. If you're going to focus your thinking in your areas of strength, you need to know what they are.

If you want to achieve great things, you need to have a great dream. If you're not sure of your dream, use your focused thinking time to help you discover it. If you're thinking has returned to a particular area time after time, you may be able to discover your dream there. Give it more focused time and see what happens. Once you find your dream, move forward without second-guessing. The younger you are, the more likely you will give your attention to many things. That's good because if you're young, you're still getting to know yourself, your strengths, and your weaknesses. If you focus your thinking on only one thing and your aspirations change, then you've wasted your best mental energy. As you get older and more experienced, the need to focus becomes more critical. The farther and higher you go, the more focused you can- and need - to be.

HOW CAN YOU STAY FOCUSED?

1. **Remove Distractions**
    Removing distractions is not a small matter in our current culture, but it's critical. How do you do it? First, by maintaining the discipline of practicing your priorities. Don't do easy things first, or hard things first, or urgent things first. Do first things first-the activities that give you the highest return. In that way, you keep the distractions to a minimum.

    Second, insulate yourself from distractions. This can include people in your life that are toxic energy vampires. I've found that I need blocks of time to think without interruptions. I've mastered the art of making myself unavailable when necessary and going off to my "thinking place" so that I can work without interruptions. Because of my responsibilities as a founder of three companies, however, I am always aware of the tension between my need to remain accessible to others as a leader, and my need to withdraw from them to think. The best way to resolve the tension is to understand the value of both activities.

    My advice to you is to place value on and give attention to both. If you naturally withdraw, then make sure to get out among people more often. If you're always on the go and very withdrawn from thinking time, then remove yourself periodically so that you can unleash the potential of focused thinking. And wherever you are, be there!

2. Make Time for Focused Thinking

Once you have a place to think, you need the time to think. Because of the fast pace of our culture, people tend to multi-task, but that's not always a good idea. Switching from task to task can cost you up to 40 percent efficiency. According to researchers, "If you're trying to accomplish many things at the same time, you'll get more done by focusing on one task at a time, not by switching constantly from one task to another."

One way to gain time for focused thinking is to impose upon yourself a rule that one company implemented: Don't allow yourself to look at email until after 10 A.M. Instead, focus your energies on your number one priority. Put one-productive time waster on hold, so that you can create thinking time for yourself.

3. Set Goals

I believe goals are important. The mind will not focus until it has clear objectives. But the purpose of goals is to focus your attention and give you direction, not to identify a final destination. As you think about your goals, note that they should be:

- Clear enough to be keep in focus

- Close enough to be achieved

- Helpful enough to change lives

Those guidelines will get you going. And be sure to write down your goals. If they're not written, I can almost guarantee that they're not focused enough. Even if you look back years from now and think your goals were too small, they will have served their purpose—if they provide you with direction.

4. Question Your Progress

Take a good look at yourself from time to time to see whether you are actually making progress. That is the most accurate measure of whether you are making the best use of focused thinking. Ask yourself, "*Am I seeing a return for my investment of focused thinking time? Is what I am doing getting me closer to my goals? Am I headed in a direction that helps me to fulfill my commitments, maintain my priorities, and realize my dreams?*"

Excuses are Well Planned Lies

If you can't get rid of the skeleton in your closet,
you'd best teach it to dance.
- George Bernard Shaw

Upside Down Thinking

If you're not as creative as you would like to be, you can change your way of thinking. Creative thinking isn't necessarily original thinking. Most often, creative thinking is a composite of other thoughts discovered along the way. Even the great artists, whom we consider highly original, learned from their masters, modeled their work on that of others, and brought together a host of ideas and styles to create their own work. Study art, and you will see threads that run through the work of all artists and artistic movements, connecting them to the artists who went before them.

CHARACTERISTIC OF UPSIDE DOWN THINKERS

Perhaps you're not even sure what I mean when I ask whether you are an Upside Down thinker. Consider some characteristics that creative thinkers have in common:

Upside Down Thinkers Value Ideas

Zig Ziglar observed, "Highly creative people are dedicated to ideas. They don't rely on their talent alone; they rely on their discipline. Their imagination is like a second skin. They know how to manipulate it to its fullest." Creativity is about having ideas-lots of them.   You will have ideas only if you value ideas.

Upside Down Thinkers Explore Options

I've yet to meet a creative thinker who didn't have options. Exploring a multitude of possibilities helps to stimulate the imagination, and imagination is crucial to creativity. As Albert Einstein put it, "Imagining is more important than knowledge." People who know me well will tell you what I place a very high value on. Why? Because they provide the key to finding the best answer- not the only answer.   Good thinkers come up with the best answers.

They create backup plans that provide them with alternatives. They enjoy
freedom that others do not possess, and they will influence and lead others.

Upside Down Thinkers Embrace Ambiguity

Creative people don't feel the need to stamp out uncertainty. They see all
kinds of inconsistencies and gaps in life, and they often take delight in
exploration of those gaps-or in using their imagination to fill them in.

Upside Down Thinkers Celebrate the Offbeat

"There is a correlation between the creative and the screwball. So we must
suffer the screwball gladly." To foster creativity in yourself or others, be
willing to tolerate a little oddness.

Upside Down Thinkers Connect the Unconnected

Because creativity utilizes the ideas of others, there's great value in being able
to connect one idea to another-especially to seemingly unrelated ideas.
"Creativity is especially expressed in the ability to make connections, to make
associations, to turn things around and express them in a new way."

Creating additional thoughts is like taking a trip on an airplane. You may
know where you are going, but only as you move toward your destination can
you see and experience things in a way not possible before you started.
Creative thinking works something like this:

THINK -> COLLECT -> CREATE -> CORRECT -> CONNECT

Once you being to think, you are free to collect. You ask yourself: *What
material relates to his thought?* Once you have the material, you ask: *What
ideas can make the thought better?* That can start taking an idea to the next
level. After that, you can correct or refine it by asking: *What changes can
make these ideas better?* Finally, you connect the ideas by positioning them in
the right context to make the thought complete and powerful.

Upside Down Thinkers Don't Fear Failure

Upside down thinking demands the ability to be unafraid of failure because creativity equals failure. You may be surprised to hear such a statement, but it's true.   Creativity requires a willingness to look stupid. It means getting out on a limb-knowing that the limb often breaks! Creative people know these things and still keep searching for new ideas. They just don't let the ideas that don't work prevent them from coming up with more ideas that do work.

WHY YOU SHOULD DISCOVER THE JOY OF UPSIDE DOWN THINKING

Creativity can improve a person's quality of life. Here are five specific things creative thinking has the potential to do for you:

· Upside Down Thinking Adds Value to Everything

Would you enjoy a limitless reserve of ideas that you could draw upon at any time? That's what creative thinking gives you. For that reason, no matter what you are currently able to do, creativity can increase your capabilities. Upside down thinking is being able to see what everybody else has seen and think what nobody else has thought, so that you can do what nobody else has done. Sometimes creative thinking lies along the lines of invention, where you break new ground. At other times, it moves along the lines of innovation which helps you to do old things in a new way. But either way, it's seeing the world through sufficiently new eyes, so that new solutions appear. That always adds value.

· Upside Down Thinking Compounds

Perhaps more than any other kinds of thinking, upside down thinking builds on itself and increases the creativity of the thinker. The more you use, the more you have. Sadly, too often creativity is smothered rather than nurtured. There has to be a climate in which new ways of thinking, perceiving, and questioning are encouraged. If you cultivate creative thinking in an environment that nurtures creativity, there's no telling what kind of ideas you can come up with.

· Upside Down Thinking Draws People to You and Your Ideas

Upside down thinking is intelligence having fun. People admire intelligence, and they are always attracted to fun-so the combination is fantastic. If you cultivate creativity, you will become more attractive to other people, and they will be drawn to you.

· Upside Down Thinking Helps You Learn More

The joy of not knowing it all refers to the realization that we seldom, if ever, have all the answers; we always have the ability to generate more solutions to just about any problem. Upside down thinking is being able to see or imagine a great deal of opportunity to life's problems. Creativity is having options.

It almost seems too obvious to say, but if you are always actively seeking new ideas, you will learn. Creativity is teaching ability. It's seeing more solutions than problems, and the greater the quantity of thoughts, the greater the chance for learning something new.

· Upside Down Thinking Challenges the Status Quo

If you desire to improve your world — or even your own situation — then creativity will help you. The status quo and creativity are incompatible. Creativity and innovation always walk hand in hand.

HOW TO DISCOVER THE JOB OF UPSIDE DOWN THINKING

At this point you may be saying, "Okay, I'm convinced that upside down thinking is important, but how do I find the creativity within me? How do I discover the joy of creative thought?" Here are five ways to do it:

1. Remove Upside Down Thinking Killers

Take a look at the following phrases. They are almost guaranteed to kill creative thinking any time you hear (or think) them:

- I'm not a creative person.

- Follow the rules.

- Don't ask questions.

- Don't be different.

- Stay within the lines.

- There is only one way.

- Don't be foolish.

- Be practical.

- Be serious.

- Think of your image.

- That's not logical.

- It's not practical.

- It's never been done.

- It can't be done.

- It didn't work for them.

- We tried that before.

- It's too much work.

- We can't afford to make a mistake.

- It will be too hard to administer.

- We don't have the time.

- We don't have the money.

- Yes, but _

- Play is frivolous.

- Failure is final.

If you think you have a great idea, don't let anyone talk you out of it, even if it sounds foolish. Don't let yourself (or anyone else) subject you to creativity killers. After all, you can't do something new and exciting if you force yourself to stay in the same old rut. Don't just work harder at the same old thing. Make a change!

2.   Think Upside Down by Asking the Right Questions

Wrong questions shut down the process of creative thinking. They direct thinkers down the same *old* path, or they chide them into believing that thinking isn't necessary at all. To stimulate creative thinking, ask yourself questions such as –

- Why must it be done *this* way?

- What is the root problem?

- What are the underlying issues?

- What does this remind me of?

- What is the opposite?

- What metaphor or symbol helps to explain it?

- Why is it important?

- What is the *hardest* or *most expensive* way to do it?

- Who has a different perspective on this?

- What happens if we *don't* do it at all?

You get the idea-and you can probably come up with better questions yourself.

3.   Develop an Upside Down Thinking Environment

Negative environments kill thousands of great ideas every minute. A creative environment, on the other hand, becomes like a greenhouse where ideas get seeded, sprout up, and flourish. A creative environment:

- ***Encourages Creativity***: When innovation and good thinking are openly encouraged and rewarded, then people see that they have permission to be creative.

- ***Places a High Value on Trust among Team Members and Individuality***: Creativity always risks failure. That's why trust is so important to creative people. In the creative process, trust comes from people working together, from knowing that people on the team have experience launching successful, creative ideas, and from the assurance that creative ideas won't go to waste because they will be implemented.

- ***Embrace Those Who Are Creative***: Pull people into brainstorming sessions. People look forward to an invitation to such meetings because the time will be filled with energy, ideas, and laughter. And the odds are high that a new project, seminar, or business strategy will result. When that happens, they also know a party's coming!

- ***Focuses on Innovation, Not Just Invention***: I heard the definition of creativity is the logical combination of two or more existing elements that result in a new concept. The best way to make a living with your imagination is to develop innovative applications, not imagine completely new concepts. Creative people say, "Give me a good idea, and I'll give you a better idea!"

- ***Is Willing to Let People Go Outside the Lines***: Most people automatically stay within lines, even if those lines have been arbitrarily drawn or are terribly out of date. Remember, most limitations we face are not imposed on us by others; we place them on ourselves. Lack of creativity often falls into that category. If you want to be more creative, challenge boundaries.

- ***Appreciates the Power of a Dream***: A creative environment promotes the freedom of a dream. A creative environment encourages the use of a blank sheet of paper and the question, "If we could draw a picture of what we want to accomplish, what would that look like?" Goals may give focus, but dreams give power. Dreams expand the world. That is why James Allen suggested that "dreamers are the saviors of the world."

The more creativity-friendly you can make your environment, the more potential it has to become creative.

4. Spend time with Other People who Think Upside Down

What if the place you work has an environment hostile to creativity, and you possess little ability to change it? One possibility is to change jobs, but what if you desire to keep working there despite the negative environment? Your best option is to find a way to spend time with other positive people.

Thinking Upside Down is contagious. Have you ever noticed what happens during a good brainstorming session? One person throws out an idea. Another person uses it as a springboard to discover another idea. Someone else takes it in yet another, even better direction. Then somebody grabs hold of it and takes it to a whole new level. The interplay of ideas can be electric.

It's a fact that you begin to think like the people you are with most. The more time you can spend with creative people engaging in creative activities, the more creative you will become.

5. Get Out of Your Box - Think Upside Down and Live Right-side Up

Upside Down thinkers know that they must repeatedly break out of the "box" of their own history and personal limits in order to experience creative breakthroughs.

The most effective way to help yourself get out of the box is to expose yourself to new paradigms. One way you can do that is by traveling to new places. Explore other cultures, countries, and tradition. Find out how people very different from you live and think. Another way is to read on new subjects. I'm naturally curious and love to learn, but I still have a tendency to read books only on my favorite subjects, such as leadership. I sometimes have to force myself to read books that broaden my thinking because I know it's worth it. If you want to break out of your own box, get into somebody else's. Read broadly.

Many people mistakenly believe that if individuals aren't born with creativity, they will never be creative. But you can see from the many strategies and examples I've given that creativity can be cultivated in the right supportive environment.

Realistic Thinking

REALITY CHECK

Reality is the difference between what we wish for and what is. It took some time for me to evolve into a realist thinker. The process went in phases. First, I did not engage in realistic thinking at all. After a while, I realized that it was necessary, so I began to engage in it occasionally. (I didn't like it, though, because I thought it was too negative. So any time I could delegate it, I did.) Eventually, I found that I *had* to engage in realistic thinking if I was going to solve problems and learn from my mistakes. And in time, I became willing to think realistically *before* I got in trouble and make it a continual part of my life. Today, I encourage my key leaders to think realistically. We make realistic thinking the foundation of our business because we derive certainty and security from it.

WHY YOU SHOULD RECOGNIZE THE IMPORTANCE OF REALISTIC THINKING

If you're a naturally optimistic person, as I am, you may not possess great desire to become a more realistic thinker. Cultivating the ability to be realistic in your thinking will not undermine your faith in people, nor will it lessen your ability to see and seize opportunities. Instead, it will add value to you in other ways:

1. **Realistic Thinking Minimizes Downside Risk**

    Actions always have consequences; realistic thinking helps you to determine what those consequences could be. And that's crucial, because only by recognizing and considering consequences can you plan for them. If you plan for the worst-case scenario, you can minimize the downside risk.

2. **Realistic Thinking Gives You a Target and Game Plan**

    I've known business people who were not realistic thinkers. Here's the good news: they were very positive and had a high degree of hope for their business. Here's the bad news: *hope is not a strategy*.

    Realistic thinking leads to excellence in leadership and management because it requires people to face reality. They begin to define their target and develop a game plan to hit it. When people engage in realistic thinking, they also begin to simplify practices and procedures which results in better efficiency.

Truthfully, in business, only a few decisions are important. Realistic thinkers understand the difference between the important decisions and those that are merely necessary in the normal course of business. The decisions that matter relate directly to your purpose. James Allen was right when he wrote, "Until thought is linked with purpose, there is not intelligent accomplishment."

3. Realistic Thinking is a Catalyst for Change

People who rely on hope for their success rarely make change a high priority. If you have only hope, you imply that achievement and success are out of your hands. It's a matter of luck or chance. Why bother changing?

Realistic thinking can dispel that kind of wrong attitude. There's nothing like staring reality in the face to make a person recognize the need for change. Change alone doesn't bring growth, but you cannot have growth without change.

4. Realistic Thinking Provides Security

Any time you have thought through the worst that can happen, and you have developed contingency plans to meet it, you become more confident and secure. It's reassuring to know that you are unlikely to be surprised. Disappointment is the difference between excessive hope and reality. Realistic thinking minimizes the difference between the two.

5. Realistic Thinking Gives You Credibility

Realistic thinking helps people to buy in to the leader and his or her vision. Leaders continually surprised by the unexpected soon lose credibility with their followers. On the other hand, leaders who think realistically and plan accordingly position their organizations to win. That gives their people confidence in them.

6. Realistic Thinking Provides a Foundation to Build On

Thomas Edison observed, "The value of a good idea is in using it." The bottom line on realistic thinking is that it helps you to make an idea usable by taking away the "wish" factor. Most ideas and efforts don't accomplish their intended results because they rely too much on what we wish, rather than what is.

You can't build a house in midair; it needs a solid foundation. Ideas and plans are the same. They need something concrete on which to build. Realistic thinking provides that solid foundation.

7. Realistic Thinking Is a Friend to Those in Trouble

If creativity is what you would do if you were unafraid of the possibility of failure, then reality is dealing with failure if it does happen. Realistic thinking gives you something concrete to fall back on during times of trouble, which can be very reassuring. Certainty in the midst of uncertainty brings stability.

8. Realistic Thinking Brings the Dream to Fruition

If you don't get close enough to a problem, you can't tackle it. If you don't take a realist look at your dream-and what it will take to accomplish it-you will never achieve it. Realistic thinking helps to pave the way for bringing any dream to fruition.

The Way You Live is How You Lead

"Most people spend more time planning their summer vacation than planning their lives." Source Unknown

When you hear the words "strategic thinking," what comes to mind? Do visions of business plans dance in your head? Do you conjure up marketing plans, the kind that can turn a company around? Strategic thinking can make a positive impact on any area of life.

PLAN YOUR LIFE, LIVE YOUR PLAN

I've observed that most people try to plan their lives one day at a time. They wake up, make up their to-do list, and dive into action. Fewer individuals plan their lives one week at a time. They review their calendar for the week, check their appointments, review their goals, and then get to work.

WHY YOU SHOULD RELEASE THE POWER OF UPSIDE DOWN THINKING

Upside Down thinking helps me to plan, to become more efficient, to maximize my strengths, and to find the most direct path toward achieving any objective. The benefits of strategic thinking are numerous. Here are a few of the reasons you should adopt it as one of your thinking tools:

1. **Upside Down Thinking Simplifies the Difficult**

   Upside Down strategic thinking takes complex issues and long-term objectives, which can be very difficult to address, and breaks them down into manageable sizes. Anything becomes simpler when it has a plan!

   Upside Down strategic thinking can also help you simplify the management of everyday life. I do that by using systems which are nothing more than good strategies repeated. Just about any difficult task can be made simpler with strategic thinking.

2. **Upside Down Thinking Prompts you to Ask the Right Questions**

   Do you want to break down complex or difficult issues? Then ask questions… the right ones.

   Direction: What should we do next? Why?

   · *Organization*: Who is responsible for what? Who is responsible for whom? Do we have the right people in the right places?

- *Cash*: What is our projected income, expenses, net? Can we afford it? How can we afford it?

- *Tracking*: Are we on target?

- *Overall Evaluation*: Are we achieving the quality we expect and demand of ourselves?

- *Refinement*: How can we be more effective and more efficient (move toward the ideal)?

These may not be the only questions you need to ask to begin formulating a strategic plan, but they are certainly a good start.

3. Upside Down Thinking Prompts Customization

All good Upside Down thinkers are precise in their thinking. They try to match the strategy to the problem because strategy isn't a one-size- fits-all proposition. Sloppy or generalized thinking is an enemy of achievement. The intention to customize in strategic thinking forces a person to go beyond vague ideas and engage in specific ways to go after a task or problem. It sharpens the mind.

4. Upside Down Thinking Prepares You Today for an Uncertain Tomorrow

Upside Down thinking is the bridge that links where you are to where you want to be. It gives direction and credibility today and increases your potential for success tomorrow.

Upside Down Thinking Reduces the Margin of Error

Any time you shoot from the hip or go into a totally reactive mode, you increase your margin for error. It's like a golfer stepping up to a golf ball and hitting it before lining up the shot. Misaligning a shot by just a few degrees can send the ball a hundred yards off target. Strategic thinking lines up your actions with your objectives, just as lining up a shot in golf helps you to put the ball closer to the pin.

5. Upside Down Thinking Gives You Influence with Others

The one with the plan is the one with the power. It doesn't matter in what kind of activity you're involved. People want to follow a leader who has demonstrated social proof. If you practice strategic thinking, others will listen to you, and you will want to follow you. If you possess a position of leadership in an organization, strategic thinking is essential. People want to like, know, and trust you.

HOW TO RELEASE THE POWER OF UPSIDE DOWN THINKING

To become a better Upside Down thinker to formulate and implement plans that will achieve the desired objective, take the following guidelines to heart:

1.   **Break Down the Issue**

   The first step-in Upside-Down thinking is to break down an issue into smaller, more manageable parts so that you can focus on them more effectively. How you do it is not as important as just doing it. You might break an issue down by function. That's what automotive innovator Henry Ford did when he created the assembly line, and that's why he said, "Nothing is particularly hard if you divide it into small jobs."

   How you break down an issue is up to you-whether it's by function, timetable, responsibility, purpose, or some other method. The point is that you need to break it down. Only one person in a million can juggle the whole thing in his head and think strategically to create solid, viable plans.

2.   **Ask Why Before How**

   When most people begin using Upside Down thinking to solve a problem or plan a way to meet an objective, they often make the mistake of jumping the gun and trying immediately to figure out how to accomplish it. Instead of asking how, they should first ask why. If you jump right into problem solving mode, how are you going to know all the issues?

   Asking why helps you to think about all the reasons for decisions. It helps you to open your mind to possibilities and opportunities. The size of an opportunity often determines the level of resources and effort that you must invest. Big opportunities allow for big decisions.

3.   **Identify the Real Issues and Objectives**

   Too many people rush to solutions, and as a result they end up solving the wrong problem. To avoid that, the power of asking exposes the real issues that challenge all of your assumptions. Collect information even after you think you've identified the issue. You may still have to act with incomplete data, but you don't want to jump to a conclusion before you gather enough information to begin identifying the real issue. Once the real issues are identified, the solutions are often simple.

4. Review Your Resources

A strategy that doesn't take into account resources is doomed to failure. Take an inventory. How much time do you have? How much money? What kids of materials, supplies, or inventory do you have? What are your other assets? What liabilities or obligations will come into play? Which people on the team can make an impact? You know your own organization and profession. Figure out what resources you have at your disposal.

5. Develop Your Plan

How you approach the planning process depends greatly on your profession and the size of the challenge that you're planning to tackle, so it's difficult to recommend many specifics. However, no matter how you go about planning, take this advice: start with the obvious. When you tackle an issue or plan that way, it brings unity and consensus to the team because everyone sees those things. Obvious elements build mental momentum and initiate creativity and intensity. The best way to create a road to the complex is to build on the fundamentals.

6. Put the Right People in the Right Place

It's critical that you include your team as part of your strategic thinking. Before you can implement your plan, you must make sure that you have the right people in place. Even the best strategic thinking won't help if you don't take into account the people part of the equation. Look at what happens if you miscalculate:

> **Wrong Person**: Problems instead of Potential
>
> **Wrong Place**: Frustration instead of Fulfillment
>
> **Wrong Plan**: Grief instead of Growth

Everything comes together, however, when you put together all three elements: the right person, the right place, and the right plan.

Thinking What is Possible

People who embrace possibility thinking are capable of accomplishing tasks that seem impossible because they believe in solutions. Here are several reasons why you should become a possibility thinker:

1. Possibility Thinking Increases Your Possibilities

When you believe you can do something difficult—and you succeed-many doors open for you.

Possibility Thinking Draws Opportunities and People to You

Being a possibility thinker can create new opportunities and attract people. People who think big attract big people to them. If you want to achieve big things, you need to become a possibility thinker.

2. Possibility Thinking Increases Others' Possibilities

Elephant thinkers who make things happen also create possibilities for others. That happens, in part, because it's contagious. You can't help but become more confident and think bigger when you're around possibility thinkers.

3. Possibility Thinking Allows You to Dream Big

No matter what your profession, possibility thinking can help you to broaden your horizons and dream bigger dreams.   Les Brown says "Big thinkers are specialists in creating positive, forward-looking, optimistic pictures in their own minds and in the minds of others." If you embrace possibility thinking, your dream will go from molehill to mountain size, and because you believe in possibilities, you put yourself in position to achieve them.

4. Possibility Thinking makes it Possible to Rise above Average

When everybody else goes right, I go left. When oil prices went through the roof, Honda was ordered to make their cars more fuel efficient. Honda asked a group of senior engineers to drastically reduce the weight of cars they were designing. They worked on the problem and searched for solutions, but they finally concluded that making lighter cars couldn't be done, would be too expensive, and would present too many safety concerns. They couldn't get out of the rut of their average thinking.

What was their solution? They gave the problem to a group of less-experienced engineers. The new group found ways to reduce the weight of the company's automobiles by hundreds of pounds. Because they thought that solving the problem was possible, it was. Every time you remove the label of impossible from a task, you raise your potential from average to off the charts.

5. **Possibility Thinking Gives You Energy**

   A direct correlation exists between possibility thinking and the level of a person's energy. Who gets energized by the prospect of losing? If you know something can't succeed, how much time and energy are you willing to give it? Nobody goes looking for a lost cause. You invest yourself in what you believe can succeed. When you embrace possibility thing, you believe in what you're doing and that gives you energy.

6. **Possibility Thinking Keeps You from Giving Up**

   Above all, possibility thinkers believe they can succeed. Denis Waitley, author of *The Psychology of Winning*, says, "The winners in life think constantly in terms of 'I can, I will and I am.' Losers, on the other hand, concentrate their waking thoughts on what they should have done, or what they don't do." If you believe you can't do something, then it doesn't matter how hard you try because you've already lost. If you believe you can do something, you have already won much of the battle.

HOW TO FEEL THE ENERGY OF POSSIBILITY THINKING

If you are a naturally positive person who already embraces possibility thinking, then you're already tracking with me. However, some people, rather than being optimistic, are naturally negative or cynical. They believe that possibility thinkers are naive or foolish. If you're thinking runs toward pessimism, let me ask you a question: *How many highly successful people do you know who are continually negative? How many impossibility thinkers are you acquainted with who achieve big things?* None!

People with an "it-can't-be-done" mindset have two choices. They can expect the worst and continually experience it; or they can change their thinking. That's what Steve Jobs did. Believe it or not, even though he is a possibility thinker, he is not a naturally positive person. The power of positive thinking goes a long way. Using determination and positive thinking (combined with talent and knowing your craft) may sound like a naive way of thinking,

but at the same time, it's worked for me, and it's worked for all my friends —
so I have come to believe it.

If you want possibility thinking to work for you, then begin by following these
suggestions:

1. **Stop Focusing on the Impossibilities**

   The first step in becoming a possibility thinker is to stop yourself
   from searching for and dwelling on what's wrong with any given
   situation.

   If possibility thinking is new to you, you're going to have to give
   yourself a lot of coaching to eliminate some of the negative self-talk
   you may hear in your head. When you automatically start listing all
   the things that can go wrong or all the reasons something can't be
   done, stop yourself and say, "Don't go there." Then ask, "What's
   right about this?" That will help to get you started. And if negativity
   is a really big problem for you, and pessimistic things come out of
   your mouth before you've even thought them through, you may need
   to enlist the aid of a friend or family member to alert you every time
   you utter negative ideas.

2. **Look for Possibilities in Every Situation**

   Becoming a possibility thinker is more than just refusing to let
   yourself be negative. It's something more. It's looking for positive
   possibilities despite the circumstances. It doesn't take a genius IQ or
   twenty years of experience to find the possibility in every situation.
   All it takes is the right attitude, and anybody can cultivate that.

3. **Dream One Size Bigger**

   One of the best ways to cultivate a possibility mind-set is to prompt
   yourself to dream one size bigger than you normally do. Let's face it:
   most people dream too small. They don't think big enough. Henry
   Curtis advised, "Make your plans as fantastic as you like, because
   twenty-five years from now, they will seem mediocre. Make your
   plans ten times as great as you first planned, and twenty-five years
   from now you will wonder why you did not make them fifty times as
   great."

   If you push yourself to dream more expansively, to imagine your
   organization one size bigger, to make your goals at least a step

beyond what makes you comfortable, you will be forced to grow, and it will set you up to believe in greater possibilities.

4. Question the Status Quo

Most people want their lives to keep improving, yet they value peace and stability at the same time. People often forget that you can't improve and still stay the same. Growth means change. Change requires challenging the status quo. If you want greater possibilities, you can't settle for what you have now. When you become a possibility thinker, you will face many people who will want you to give up your dream and embrace the status quo. Achievers refuse to accept the status quo.

As you begin to explore greater possibilities for yourself, your organization, or your family—and others challenge you for it—take comfort in knowing that *right now* as you read this, other possibility thinkers across the country and around the world are thinking about curing cancer, developing new energy sources, feeding hungry people and improving quality of life. They are challenging the status quo against the odds—and you should, too.

5. Find Inspiration from Great Achievers

You can learn a lot about possibility thinking by studying great achievers. I mentioned George Lucas in this chapter. Perhaps he doesn't appeal to you, or you don't like the move industry. (Personally, I'm not a big science fiction fan, but I admire Lucas as a thinker, creative visionary, and business person.) Find some achiever you admire and study them. Look for people with the attitude of Robert F. Kennedy, who popularized George Bernard Shaw's stirring statement: "Some men see things as they are and say, 'Why?' I dream of things that never were and say, 'Why not?'"

I know possibility thinking isn't in style with many people. So call it what you like: the will to succeed, believe in yourself, confidence in your ability, faith. It's really true: people who believe they can't, don't. But if you believe you can, you can! That's the power of possibility thinking.

Life shrinks or expands in proportion to one's courage. - Anais Nin

Popular Thinking vs. Unpopular Thinking

Going against popular thinking can be difficult, whether you're a business person bucking company tradition, a pastor introducing new types of music to his church, a new mother rejecting old wives' tales handed down from her parents, or a teenager ignoring currently popular styles.

Many of the ideas in this book go against popular thinking. If you value popularity over good thinking, then you will severely limit your potential to learn the types of thinking encouraged by this book.

Popular thinking is---

- Too average to understand the value of good thinking,

- Too inflexible to realize the impact of changed thinking,

- Too lazy to master the process of international thinking,

- Too small to see the wisdom of elephant thinking,

- Too satisfied to unleash the potential of focused thinking,

- Too traditional to discover the joy of Thinking Upside Down,

- Too naive to recognize the importance of realistic thinking,

- Too undisciplined to release the power of strategic thinking,

- Too limiting to feel the energy of possibility thinking,

- Too proud to encourage the participation of shared thinking,

- Too self-absorbed to experience the satisfaction of unselfish thinking, and

- Too uncommitted to enjoy the return of bottom-line thinking.

If you want to become a good thinker, then start preparing yourself for the possibility of becoming unpopular.

WHY YOU SHOULD QUESTION THE ACCEPTANCE OF POPULAR THINKING

1. Popular Thinking Sometimes Means Not Thinking

Good thinking is hard work. If it were easy, everybody would be a good thinker. Unfortunately, many people try to live life the easy way. They don't want to do the hard work of thinking or pay the price of success. It's easier to do what other people do and hope that *they* thought it out. When people blindly follow a trend, they're not doing their own thinking.

Popular Thinking Offers False Hope

Many people look for safety and security in popular thinking. They figure that if a lot of people are doing something, then it must be right. It must be a good idea. If most people accept it, then it probably represents fairness, equality, compassion and sensitivity, right? Not necessarily. Popular thinking said the earth was the center of the universe, yet Copernicus studied the stars and planets, and proved mathematically that the earth and the other planets in our solar system revolved around the sun. Popular thinking said surgery didn't require clean instruments, yet Joseph Lister studied the high death rates in hospitals and introduced antiseptic practices that immediately saved lives. Popular thinking put the Nazis into power in Germany, yet Hitler's regime murdered millions and nearly destroyed Europe.

Sometimes it's painfully obvious that popular thinking isn't good and right. Other times it's less evident. For example, consider the staggering number of people in the United States who have run up large amounts of debt on their credit cards. Anyone who is financially astute will tell you that's a bad idea. Yet millions follow right along with the popular thinking of buy now, pay later. And so they pay, and pay, and pay.

Popular Thinking Is Slow to Embrace Change

Popular thinking loves the status quo. It puts its confidence in the idea of the moment and holds on to it with all its might. As a result, it resists change and dampens innovation. We must stop assuming that a thing which has never been done before probably cannot be done at all.

2. Popular Thinking Brings Only Average Results

The bottom line? Popular thinking brings mediocre results. Popular =
Normal = Average. It's the least of the best and the best of the least.
We limit our success when we adopt popular thinking which will not
take us to the power of asking which will and can change our lives. It
represents putting in the least energy to just get by. You must reject
common thinking if you want to accomplish uncommon results.

HOW TO QUESTION THE ACCEPTANCE OF POPULAR THINKING

Popular thinking has often proved to be wrong and limiting. Questioning it
isn't necessarily hard, once you cultivate the habit of doing so. The difficulty
is in getting started. Begin by doing the following things:

1. Think Before You Follow

Many individuals follow others almost automatically. Sometimes
they do so because they desire to take the path of least resistance.
Other times, they fear rejection, or they believe there's wisdom in
doing what everyone else does. But if you want to succeed, you need
to think about what's best, not what's popular.

Challenging popular thinking requires a willingness to be unpopular
and go outside of the norm. Following the tragedy of September 11,
2001, for example, few people willingly chose to travel by plane.
Guess what? I was on a plane to Hawaii September 13, 2001, and it
was the first flight out of Los Angeles since the tragedy on September
11, 2001, but that was the best time to travel: crowds were down,
security was up, and airlines were cutting prices. When I arrived in
Hawaii, there was nobody on the beach. It looked like a deserted
island. I used that as an opportunity.

As you begin to think against the grain of popular thinking, remind
yourself that:

- Unpopular thinking, even when resulting in success, is largely
  underrated, unrecognized, and misunderstood.

- Unpopular thinking contains the seeds of vision and opportunity.

- Unpopular thinking is required for all progress.

The next time you feel ready to conform to popular thinking on an issue, stop and think. You may not want to create change for its own sake, but you certainly don't want to blindly follow just because you haven't thought about what's best.

2. Appreciate Thinking Different from Your Own

One of the ways to embrace innovation and change is to learn to appreciate how others think. As you strive to challenge popular thinking, spend time with people with different backgrounds, education levels, professional experiences, personal interests, etc. You will think like the people with whom you spend the most time. If you spend time with people who think out of the box, you're more likely to challenge popular thinking and break new.

3. Try New Things in New Ways

When was the last time you did something for the first time? Do you avoid taking risks or trying new things? One of the best ways to get out of the rut of your own thinking is to innovate. You can do that in little, everyday ways: drive to work a different way from normal; order an unfamiliar dish at your favorite restaurant; ask a different colleague to help you with a familiar project. Take yourself off of autopilot.

Unpopular thinking asks questions and seeks options. In 1997, my three companies moved to Atlanta, Georgia. It's a great city, but traffic at peak times can get crazy. Immediately after moving here, I began looking for and testing alternative routes to desired destinations, so that I would not be caught in traffic. From my house to the airport, for example, I have discovered and used nine routes within eight miles and twelve minutes from one another. Often, I am amazed to see people sitting on the freeway when they could be moving forward on an alternative route. What is the problem? Too many people have not tried new things in new ways. It is true: most people are more satisfied with old problems than committed to finding new solutions.

How you go about doing new things in new ways is not as important as making sure you do it. (Besides, if you try to do new things in the same way that everyone else does, are you really going against popular thinking?) Get out there and do something different today.

4. Get Used to Being Uncomfortable

When it comes right down to it, popular thinking is comfortable. It's like an old recliner adjusted to all the owner's idiosyncrasies. The problem with most old recliners is that no one has *looked* at them lately. If so, they'd agree that it's time to get a new one! If you want to reject popular thinking in order to embrace achievement, you'll have to get used to being uncomfortable.

If you embrace popular thinking and make decisions based upon what works best and what is right rather than what is commonly accepted, know this: in your early years you won't be as wrong as people think you are. In your later years, you won't be as right as people think you are. And all through the years, you will be better than you thought you could be.

BENEFIT FROM TOGETHER THINKING

"Good thinkers, especially those who are also good leaders, understand the power of shared thinking. They know that when they value the thoughts and ideas of others, they receive the compounding results of shared thinking and accomplish more than they never could on their own."

Those who participate in shared thinking understand the following:

1. Together Thinking Is Faster than Solo Thinking

We live in a truly fast-paced world. To function at its current rate of speed, we can't go it alone. I think the generation of young men and women just entering the workforce sense that very strongly. Perhaps that is why they value community so highly and are more likely to work for a company they like than one that pays them well. Working with others is like giving yourself a shortcut.

If you want to learn a new skill quickly, how do you do it? Do you go off by yourself and figure it out, or do you get someone to show you how? You can always learn more quickly from someone with experience- This is why people hire me for consulting and training because I have done it and have social proof.

Together Thinking Is More Innovative than Thinking Alone

We tend to think of great thinkers and innovators as soloists, but the truth is that the greatest innovative thinking doesn't occur in a vacuum. Innovation results from collaboration. If you combine your thoughts with the thoughts of others, you will come up with thoughts you've never had!

2. Together Thinking Brings More Maturity than Thinking Alone

As much as we would like to think that we know it all, each of us is probably painfully aware of our blind spots and areas of inexperience. You've had experiences I haven't, and I've had experiences you haven't. Put us together, and we bring a broader range of personal history—and therefore, maturity—to the table. If you don't have the experience you need, hook up with someone who does.

3. Together Thinking Is Stronger than Thinking Alone

Two heads are better than one—when they are thinking in the same direction. It's like harnessing two horses to pull a wagon. Accepting good advice is but to increase one's own abilities. They are stronger pulling together than either is individually. But did you know that when they pull together, they can move more weight than the sum of what they can move individually? A synergy comes from working together. That same kind of energy comes into play when people think together.

4. Together Thinking Returns Greater Value than Solo Thinking

Because thinking together is stronger than solo thinking, it's obvious that it yields a higher return. That happens because of the compounding action of shared thinking. But it also offers other benefits. The personal return you receive from shared thinking and experiences can be great.

5. Together Thinking Is the Only Way to Have Great Thinking

I believe that every great idea begins with three or four good ideas. And most good ideas come from thinking with others.

When I was in school, teachers put the emphasis on being right and on doing better than the other students, rarely on working together to come up with good answers. Yet all the answers improve when they make the best use of everyone's thinking. If we each have one thought, and together we have two thoughts, then we always have the potential for a great thought.

HOW TO ENCOURAGE THE PARTICIPATION OF TOGETHER THINKING

Some people naturally participate in together thinking. Any time they see a problem they think, *"Who do I know who can help with this?"* Leaders tend to be that way. So do extroverts. However, you don't have to be either of those to benefit from together thinking. Use the following steps to help you improve your ability to harness together thinking:

1. Value the Ideas of Others

First, believe that the ideas of other people have value. If you don't, your hands will be tied. How do you know if you truly want input from others? Ask yourself these questions:

- **Am I emotionally secure?** People who lack confidence and worry about their status, position, or power tend to reject the ideas of others, protect their turf, and keep people at bay. Remember hurting people hurt people.

- **Do I place value on people?** You won't value the ideas of a person, if you don't value and respect the person himself or herself. Have you ever considered your conduct around people you value versus those you don't? Look at the differences:

If I Value People	If I Don't Value People
I want to spend time with them.	I don't want to be around them.
I listen to them.	I neglect to listen
I want to help them.	I don't offer them help.
I am influenced by them.	I ignore them.
I respect them.	I am indifferent.

- **Do I value the interactive process?** A wonderful synergy often occurs as the result of together thinking. It can take you places you've never been. Together thinking is only as good as the people doing the sharing.

You must open yourself up to the *idea* of sharing ideas before you will engage in the *process* of together thinking.

2. Move from Competition to Cooperation

A person who values cooperation desires to complete the ideas they have, not compete with them. If someone asks you to share ideas, focus on helping the team, not getting ahead personally. And if you are the one who brings people together to share their thoughts, praise the idea more than the source of the idea.

3. Get the Right People Around the Table

To get anything of value out of shared thinking, you need to have people around who bring something to the table. Too often we choose our brainstorming partners based on feelings of friendship or circumstances or convenience. But that doesn't help us to discover and create the ideas of the highest order. Who we invite to the table makes all the difference.

UNSELFISH THINKING IS THE KEY TO THE POWER OF ASKING

1. Unselfish Thinking Brings Personal Fulfillment

Few things in life bring greater personal rewards than helping others. Charles Shultz believed, "Getters generally don't get happiness; givers get it." Helping people brings great satisfaction. When you spend your day unselfishly serving others, at night you can lay down your head with no regrets.

If you have spent much of your life pursuing selfish gain, it is not ever too late to have a change of heart. Even the most miserable person can turn his life around and make a difference for others. When you get outside of yourself and make a contribution to others, you really begin to live.

2. Unselfish Thinking Encourages Other Virtues

When you see a four-year-old, you expect to observe selfishness. But when you see it in a forty-year-old, it's not very attractive, is it? I have experienced it and believe me it is not living on a high vibration.

Of all the qualities a person can pursue, unselfish thinking seems to make the biggest difference toward opening doors vs. closing them. I think that's because the ability to give unselfishly is so difficult. It goes against the grain of human nature. But if you can learn to think unselfishly and become a giver, then it becomes easier to develop many other virtues: gratitude, love, respect, patience, discipline, etc.

3. Unselfish Thinking Increases Quality of Life

The spirit of generosity created by unselfish thinking gives people an appreciation for life and an understanding of its higher values. Seeing those in need and giving to meet that need puts a lot of things into perspective. It increases the quality of life of the giver and the receiver.

4.   **Unselfish Thinking Creates a Legacy**

If you are successful, it becomes possible for you to leave an inheritance *for* others. But if you desire to do more, to create a legacy, then you need to leave that *in* others. When you think unselfishly and invest in others, you gain the opportunity to create a legacy that will outlive you.

THE SECRET OF HOW I HAVE BEEN SUCCESSFUL

I think most people recognize the value of unselfish thinking, and most would even agree that it's an ability they would like to develop. Many people, however, are at a lost concerning how to change their thinking. To begin cultivating the ability to think unselfishly, I recommend that you do the following:

1.   **Put Others First**

The process begins with realizing that everything is not about you! That requires humility and a shift in focus. If you want to become less selfish in your thinking, then you need to stop thinking about your wants and begin focusing on others' needs. You should look not only to your own interest, but the interest of others. This is what I teach in my branding and social media courses. It is not about you, it is about who you can help, "But Bardi, I want to make money." If you are in the mode of desperation vs. inspiration, it will not work. Changing your mindset gives you the power to ask, which will change your life. Make a mental and emotional commitment to look out for the interests of others.

2.   **Expose Yourself to Situations Where People Have Needs**

It's one thing to believe you are willing to give unselfishly. It's another to actually do it. To make the transition, you need to put yourself in a position where you can see people's needs and do something about it.

The kind of giving you do isn't important at first. You can serve at your church, make donations to a food bank, volunteer professional services, or give to a charitable organization. The point is to learn how to give and to cultivate the habit of thinking like a giver.

3. Give Quietly or Anonymously

Once you have learned to give of yourself, then the next step is to
learn to give when you cannot receive anything in return. It's almost
always easier to give when you receive recognition for it than it is
when no one is likely to know about it. The people who give in order
to receive a lot of fanfare, however, have already received any reward
they will get. There are spiritual, mental, and emotional benefits that
come only to those who give anonymously. If you've never done it
before, try it.

4. Invest in People Intentionally

The highest level of unselfish thinking comes when you give of
yourself to another person for that person's personal development or
well-being. If you're married or a parent, you know this from
personal experience. What does your spouse value most highly;
money in the bank or your time freely given? What would small
children really rather have from you: a toy or your undivided
attention? The people who love you would rather have you than what
you can give them.

If you want to become the kind of person who invests in people, then
consider others and their journey so that you can collaborate with
them. Each relationship is like a partnership created for mutual
benefit. As you go into any relationship, think about how you can
invest in the other person, so that it becomes a win-win situation.
Here is how relationships most often play out:

> I win, you lose — I win only once.
>
> You win, I lose — You win only once.
>
> We both win — We win many times.
>
> We both lose — Goody-bye, partnership!

The best relationships are win-win. Why don't more people go into
relationships with that attitude? I'll tell you why: most people want
to make sure that they win first. Unselfish thinkers, on the other
hand, go into a relationship and make sure that the other person wins
first. And that makes all the difference.

5.   Continually Check Your Motives

The hardest thing for most people is fighting their natural tendency to put themselves first. That's why it's important to continually examine your motives to make sure you're not sliding backward into selfishness.

12 Powerful Motivational Tools

That Guarantee Success

No matter how many years you spend in a classroom, or from what social class or lifestyle you come, motivation is the common factor among those who are high achievers.

Finding the tools to put meaning and purpose in your life, developing a vision, and becoming highly motivated can lead you towards a successful and exciting life.

Here are 12 motivational tools that can bring you success:

1. Recognizing obstacles and learning to remove them can make your vision a reality. The individual who is extremely motivated and successful has been motivated by a vision.

2. The quest for freedom is the basis for motivation. Total freedom is not necessarily desirable or possible, but the pursuit of that ideal is what motivates us to succeed.

3. People who develop a vision control their own life and destiny. With no vision, your life and destiny are controlled by outside forces. You must change your thinking habits in order to change your life, and you change your habits by keeping the desired results in sight.

4. Develop a major goal, but take a specified path to get there. You'll have many smaller goals to reach before you get to the final result. By learning to accomplish these smaller goals, you'll be motivated to take on the larger challenges.

5. Get into the habit of finishing what you start. An unfinished project is of no value. Leaving things unfinished is a habit that must be changed.

6. Find support through friends, acquaintances, and co-workers. If you surround yourself with motivated, visionary people, you will naturally develop the attributes that helped them get that way. Mutual interests and like-minded associates can be excellent motivational tools.

7. Another motivational tool is failure. Failure teaches us to keep trying until we get it right. No one ever became successful without prior failures. Failure is a by-product of imagination and creativity. It challenges you to take risks and teaches you to keep trying until you get it right.

8. The fear of failure is a common factor among those who procrastinate. If you want to succeed in reaching your goals, you must be willing to take a risk and lose. Many people trade joy, satisfaction, and fulfillment for a job that is considered conventional and safe.

9. The unfulfilling job is not the failure; not pursuing your dreams is the real failure. Developing a vision requires conquering your fears and finding motivation from within.

10. The power of your dreams is the primary factor in becoming motivated. Productivity will be the result of developing habits and attitudes that keep you on the right track.

11. By changing bad habits and focusing on your specific goals, motivation will come to you even when you wish you could quit, and times are tough.

12. By identifying the behaviors that you need to change, developing a vision of what you would like to achieve, and striving to attain that goal, you will become a naturally motivated, highly efficient, productive person. Here are some of the behaviors:

☐Do not let fear of failure stop you from having the freedom to choose the lifestyle and destiny you desire.

☐ Motivation is not only a learned skill; it is developed due to a need or desire to make our dreams a reality.

☐ If you want to find inner motivation, you must identify your goals and set out on an unwavering path to achieve them.

☐ Not procrastinating is perhaps one of the most important steps you can take to improve your life and become the motivated, successful person you are capable of being.

☐ Let go of your old personality and ways of doing things to change quit procrastinating and get motivated!

Shake Off
Your Chains

*"Some look at things that are and ask why. I dream
of things that never were and ask why not?"*
- George Bernard Shaw

THE KEY TO THE POWER OF ASKING

Make a conscious decision to focus on the positive

Throughout the ages, the people who use the power of asking to have referred to a place within themselves called the higher self, that place where an image of perfection exists which is continually attempting to express itself.

As individuals, we persistently get stimulating and upbeat messages to our consciousness; messages meant to protect our integrity and wholeness. Messages coming from the heart always have a complete disregard for the facts or surrounding circumstances in our lives. 99 out of every 100 people misread the signals they are constantly receiving.

Rather than viewing these images with the vision of understanding, seeing them as unique pictures that are full of power, possibility and promise, these images are considered idles, wishes, ridiculous fantasies or daydreams.

Millions of people struggle day after day, dominated by facts in their minds. These are dominated by the lack, the limitations, and the poverty which is reflected in their present results. They know why they cannot succeed, it's obvious to them, and they can prove it. The facts win over and over.

The key to the power of asking is your thinking, as I have discussed so far in this book. If the last paragraph above was a description of your way of life, release it, let it go. Begin doing what I suggest, and your compensation will be worth your effort.

You were meant to have and enjoy every good thing that life can offer.

Thoughts are things. Your thoughts are not just clouds floating in your mind. Thoughts are impulses. They are ways of energy that, as far as we can tell, penetrate all time and space. Thought is action in rehearsal.

Your thoughts are very powerful. They are real, they are measurable, and they are energy. Every single thought you have generates a change in your body. You are a product of all of the thoughts you think today, feelings you feel today, and actions you take today. These will determine your experiences tomorrow, so it is imperative that you learn to think and behave in a positive way that is in alignment with what you ultimately want to be, do, and experience in life.

YOUR THINKING WILL CHANGE YOUR SELF-IMAGE

Your entire life revolves around images. Just as every company has a corporate image, every individual also has their own *self*-image.

Psychology has isolated **the one prime cause for success or failure in life. It is the hidden self-image that you have of yourself.** It controls your mind, most as surely as your mind controls your heartbeat. To re-make your hidden self-image for success and fulfillment is to re-make your entire life.

Your success in any undertaking will never be greater than the image you have of yourself. Your self-image is your own conception of the sort of person you are. It determines what you believe you are able to accomplish. Your self-image was very likely unconsciously formed from past experiences: your success and failures, your humiliations and triumphs. This image, or opinion you have of yourself, will determine how you interpret other people's reactions to you and significantly affect your success.

No person and no circumstance on earth can prevent you from improving your self-image. The degree to which you improve the image of yourself will be in exact proportion to the amount of truth that you can honestly accept and the amount of positive change you put into engineering your new self-image.

POWER OF ASKING + YOUR ACTIONS CONTROL YOUR RESULTS

POWER OF ASKING ERRORS

You may know people who are continually struggling to improve. Salespeople whose sales are low and who are always struggling to raise their sales without success. They may be a student whose grades are always at the 'C' level, or even drop, when pushed to study harder. Many of these people are always broke; they never look overly happy; they are constantly in debt. Why? Why can't they improve? Let's analyze this situation and discover their common error.

1.   These people are trying desperately to change their END RESULT.

2.   The RESULTS in their lives will be determined by their ACTIONS.

3.   And their ACTIONS are continually being motivated by their self-image.

They are clutched by an unseen enemy because there is no understanding of self-mage which is the actual cause of their present self-image. They do not have a positive image.

POWER OF ASKING My Thoughts and Action Ideas

THE LEARNING PROCESS

You could be in the habit of skipping over the detailed part of a project, assuming the details are not overly important. Many times they may not be very important. However, that is certainly not the case in this program, *the details are vitally important*. Taking the time to complete each exercise will solidly plan a winner's image in the treasury of your subconscious mind, and your life will never be the same again.

COMMITMENT

**Make a written signed commitment
to use these pages every day for ninety days.**

<table><tr><td>

This is my binding commitment to:

Signature

</td></tr></table>

POWER OF ASKING My Thoughts and Action Ideas

BEGIN THE POWER OF ASKING PROCESS

Everything has a beginning: if you drive, you had to learn how to drive; if you type, you had to learn how. The same is true for living successfully. When you learn how to do something, you begin by learning the basics and then diligently work with those basics until you have them mastered. Although you may be impatient in the beginning because of your desire for improved results, understand that the time you invest to master the basics will pay great dividends in the long run.

Mastering the basics of thinking positive to build a better self-image is the same as laying a strong foundation upon which you build a house. When you build a better self-image, it increases your self-esteem to ask for what you want in all areas of your life.

The Basics

The basics begin with an understanding that all of the results you have been experiencing in your life have a very definite cause.

Actions - The Results You Choose

Asking vs Not Asking at All

A highly successful person uses The Power of Asking to Change their Life. Change Your Thinking will Change Your Life.

BUILDING YOUR POWER OF ASKING IMAGE

There are two phases which must be completed in the process of building a new self-image which will cause you to:

Think like a Leader

Feel like a Leader

Act like a Leader

Ask like a Leader

You must personally put each of these phases through two tests. If each phase does not pass the test, you could very easily sell yourself short and not properly complete each phase. Imagine being very hungry and going to a banquet, tasting the hors d'oeuvre, but then leaving before the main course is served.

POWER OF ASKING My Thoughts and Action Ideas

THE DREAM

Everything that has ever been accomplished by anyone was at first, and for a time, a dream. A DVD Player, the mobile phone, video games, and air travel were dreams long before they became reality. Thomas Edison HAD A DREAM, Alexander Graham Bell HAD A DREAM, the Wright Brothers DREAMED; we could go on and on.

Your first step calls for you to do the same as they did and choose your DREAM. Pick a highly successful person whom you admire and who you can emulate. You should pick someone you know or have read about who lives the way you dream of living. Use them as a model to help you mentally build your DREAM.

Name six people who are doing what you would like to do or who are living as you would like to live:

1.

2.

3.

4.

5.

6.

Now choose various aspects of their lives that appeal to you and mentally put yourself in their position.

As you do this, be aware that you can see with your inner eye, a beautiful vision — with yourself in it.

Visions are created in your conscious mind through the use of your imagination. It is very important that your fantasy or image be complete. Use as much detail as possible. You could feel that this is a foolish waste of time — do it anyway.

POWER OF ASKING My Thoughts and Action Ideas

Here are a few questions you could ask yourself about the people that you have named. The answers to these questions will help you build your dream:

How do they dress?

What do they study?

How do they manage their time?

Who do they associate with?

How do they meet and greet people?

How do you and others view them?

What income bracket are they in?

What is their personal life like?

What is their home like?

What kind of automobile do they drive?

Are they a service-oriented person?

Are they recognized in their industry?

(Make up questions which apply to your dream.)

My Dream

Paint with words the vision you see. Make a detailed, written description of your fantasy.

This is my Dream:

____

____

____

____

____

If you are not well read in the area of mind dynamics or the creative process, these various exercises could appear to be ridiculous. Nevertheless, they do work, and they will work for you. You are building a winner's self-image and becoming a positive thinker which will enable you to live the life you have been dreaming about.

Turning your DREAM into a THEORY requires a shift in your attitude. You must begin giving serious, conscious thought to your DREAM. **This is not a game…it is your life you are working with.**

AM I ABLE?

Are you ABLE to live your life in the manner which your DREAM suggests?

SUCCESSFUL THINKING + UNSELFISH THINKING + INCREASED SELF IMAGE / THE POWER TO ASK = POSITIVE ACTIONS

POWER OF ASKING

+ FOLLOWED BY ACTION

A LIFE OF FREEDOM, SUCCESS, AND THE ABILITY TO LEAVE A LEGACY

This is the point in life where every CHAMPION first separated himself from the masses. The FACTS or CIRCUMSTANCES clearly indicated they could not win, however, they ignored the facts and turned all of their conscious attention to their DREAM. The DREAM became real in their mind…it turned into a theory. The vision was so stimulating, they would only think of how they could live their dream. There was not room in their mind for thoughts of why they couldn't, and they became willing to do whatever was required to turn their THEORY into a new set of FACTS in their life.

You can do this. Just get out of your own way. There is no one alive who can even guess with any accuracy at the magnitude of your potential. You are a spiritual being. **For you, all things are possible.**

POWER OF ASKING My Thoughts and Action Ideas

5 Step
Program for Leaders

1. **Relax**

    Allocate 20 minutes three times every day: Morning. Noon. Evening. Let yourself totally relax. Clear your mind and visualize yourself living your dream and being the leader, you were called to be.

2. **Change**

    Completely review how you have been living and decide what changes must be made to become the person you have visualized yourself being in your new image. Then change them.

3. **Communicate**

    Make a list of 15 leaders you respect and would like to socialize with. Phone one every day to say hello and ask if there is any way you can help them. You will be speaking to every one of them twice a month.

4. **Ask**

    Make a list of 25 items you want to ask for, that you haven't asked for before. I will give you my list. My first question to you is this: If you only had 48 hrs. to live what would you ask for?

Here is a fourth of my list, and it has all come to fruition:

- *Michael Beckwith to write the foreword of my book.*

- *Jack Canfield to endorse my book.*

• *I have asked to send my book to places like Air 1 and KLOVE, the two largest Spiritual radio stations in the world. I called and asked whom may I send my book to. Guess what? I called, I asked, they gave me the information. If I had never had the right mindset to pick up that phone, the right self-image, I would never had asked.*

• *I have asked people whom I have seen on Oprah and other talk shows how they got on and the process.*

• *I asked Michael Beckwith, Dr. John Gray, John Assaraf, Les Brown, Good Morning America, The Today Show, and Steve Harvey if I could send them my book. My best seller Thinking Upside Down Living Rightside Up was written to transform the world.*

• *I have asked for my needs and wants from my spouse. So many of us will not ask our partners for what we want because we have these expectations. I discuss this early on in the book.*

• *I have asked for things from strangers, even though I felt stupid. I have asked for help in every area of my life, business and personal.*

• *I have asked for the New York Times Book Review to read my book and called them on the phone. I asked for the editor's name, her direct line, and address.*

• *I have asked for more money from my clients. I raised my pricing because what I do is valuable, I have social proof, and I deserve to be paid what I am worth. I have a proven track record and have gotten businesses, corporations, and entrepreneurs instant results with my branding, social media, and mindset strategies.*

"If you do not ask, the answer will always be no." - Bardi Toto

Optimism is the faith that leads to achievement. Nothing can be done without hope and confidence.
    - Helen Keller

What I deserve, and what I am going to ask for today

A DETAILED DESCRIPTION OF YOURSELF AS A LEADER

This written description of yourself **must** be in the present tense. Everything begins on a mental level before it manifests in physical results. As you make this written description, you are impregnating your winner's image into cells in your brain.

Rewrite this image weekly. You will find it will keep improving each time you rewrite it.

1. Relax

Allocate 20 minutes three times every day:
Morning…Noon…Evening…let yourself totally RELAX.
Clear your mind and visualize yourself living your dream.

This exercise is vitally important.

Real leaders are highly results-oriented individuals and always have a number of projects going at the same time. They accomplish more in a week than most people would accomplish in a month or possibly a year. They carry out their duties in a calm, confident, relaxed manner.

Relaxing is not something leaders try to do; it is the way they are. The subconscious mind is programmed to keep them in a relaxed state. Creative energy flows freely through the mind and body that is relaxed. Dynamic, creative, results-oriented ideas are built with creative energy.

When you have let yourself move into a totally relaxed state, mentally throw the electrical switch in your brain that permits the winner's image to move onto the screen of your mind. This is the image you choose to create and that you described previously. See yourself as a leader in every way; make it real—make it in the present tense. When that positive thinking dominates your mind, you are that person. The more often you practice this exercise, the more it will take root. Eventually, it will dominate your mind all of the time. You are then the winner—intellectually, spiritually, and physically.

Habits are formed by repeatedly getting emotionally involved with specific ideas.

For you to successfully form the habit of living a relaxed creative life, you must properly complete this exercise.

POWER OF ASKING My Thoughts and Action Ideas

"Tension tires...Relaxation renews."

2. Change

Completely review how you have been living and decide what changes must be made to become the person you have visualized yourself being in your new image. Then change them.

This is the one point which will require more effort than all of the others combined. Clearly understand, however, that the other points are of no value whatsoever if you do not systematically complete this exercise. Experience has taught all winners that they would not have properly completed this exercise had they not done the others. All pieces are necessary to complete the puzzle.

Here are ten areas of your life you must review. You can, and probably should, add to this list. As you review them on the following pages, clearly indicate the changes you will make and when you will initiate the change:

1. Personal Appearance

2. Personal Life

3. Social Life

4. Personal Development Program

5. Health

6. Working Habits

7. Attitude

8. Time Management

9. Business Associates

10. Leadership Abilities

1.   Personal Appearance: **Completion Date**: within
      7 days

Changes I Will Make

I will visit an image consultant who has established a professional reputation. I will explain what I intend to accomplish and ask for professional advice. I want to be recognized by my peers as one of the best dressed people they know.

"You cannot get new results with old habits.

Change is essential for growth." ~unknown

1. Asking for my needs and wants in my personal life

Changes I WILL make: Completion Date:

____

____

____

____

____

____

____

____

2. Asking for my needs and wants in my social life

Changes I WILL make: Completion Date:

____

____

____

____

____

____

____

____

3. *Power of Asking* Coaching Program

Changes I WILL make: Completion Date:

____

____

____

____

____

____

4. Asking for my needs and wants for good health

Changes I WILL make: Completion Date:

____

____

____

____

____

____

5. Asking for my needs and wants for my working habits

Changes I WILL make: Completion Date:

____

____

____

____

____

____

6. Asking for my needs and wants to have an attitude of gratitude

Changes I WILL make: Completion Date:

____

____

____

____

____

____

____

7. Asking for my needs and wants for time management

Changes I WILL make: Completion Date:

____

____

____

____

____

____

____

8. Asking for my needs and wants with my business associates

Changes I WILL make: Completion Date:

____

____

____

____

____

____

____

9. Asking for my needs and wants to increase my leadership abilities

Changes I WILL make: Completion Date:

____

____

____

____

____

____

____

10. Asking for my needs and wants for my business

Changes I WILL make: Completion Date:

____

____

____

____

____

____

____

____

____

____

____

____

____

____

____

____

____

____

____

____

____

____

____

____

____

____

____

____

____

____

____

____

____

____

____

____

3. Listen

Play POSITIVE audios in your car. Clear your car of all audios or music that is not positive. Play these positive audios constantly every time you are in your car for the next 90 days.

It leaves you with the choice of listening to only those suggestions you require for the development of a positive image. That truly is what you want, the proper theories and suggestions for you to plant in your subconscious mind.

Whenever you are in your car, play these for 90 days. Play them until you can talk along with the messages. Your mind may wander as the audio is playing, and that's okay... The ideas on the audios will still have a positive effect on your thoughts and actions.

Repetition... Repetition... Repetition...

It is the first law of learning.

4. Communicate

Make a list of 15 Leaders you respect and would like to socialize with. Message or phone one every day to say hello and ask if there is any way you can help them. You will be speaking to every one of them twice a month.

Making contact even on Instagram and staying in touch with other winners is a deeply rooted habit winners have firmly established. You don't have to be concerned with what they will do for you, just think of how you can help them. This is an orderly universe you are a part of; the universe will always return to you what you give to it. People with a winner's image operate within a network; they are continually helping one another.

Send them a a friendly note, to help them. If you can steer business their way, do it. Consciously and deliberately build yourself an excellent network of highly successful people.

5.   Saving The Best for Last - Just Ask

Make a list of 25 items you want to ask for that you haven't asked for before. I will give you my list. My first question to you is this: If you only had 48 hours to live, what would you ask for?

Watch out for the imposters in your head that will try to stop you. Tell them to go away, or call your mentor. My students who are in The *Power of Asking* coaching program, call me. However, since they have implemented the *Power of Asking* in their business and their personal lives, they are busy succeeding, creating, abundance, and making a difference in the world. These are the people who ask and take action.

Asking for What You Want in Business

How do we appropriately ask for what we want from others in the business world? Is there a right way and a wrong way? I am approached somewhat frequently with requests for help from both professionals in my network and people I don't know. Some requests evoke an immediate favorable response from me. Some make me pause and reflect before I respond, and still others make me cringe because of the way I am approached. Why the broad spectrum of reactions?

Before beginning this post, I chatted with a few other professionals about their experiences on this topic and analyzed the last several requests for assistance I have received. What I learned from this exercise is that many people seeking help often lack self-awareness and fail to recognize how they come across to others. They often have a genuine need for help, but the way their need is communicated comes across one-sided and self-serving.

BEST Practices for Seeking Help

• Be courteous. I am sometimes amazed at the lack of common courtesy in the requests I receive. "Please" and "thank you" and "I am grateful" should be a given, but many times, aren't.

• Offer help before asking for help. An offshoot of courtesy is to make sure the person receiving the request knows you desire to help them as well.

• Provide context. How did you find me (if we do not know each other)? Why do you think I can help you?

• Do your homework. Know as much as possible about the person you are seeking help from before reaching out. Doing research and sharing some of it in your communication makes your approach seem less random and will evoke a warmer response.

• Spotlight the connections. How are you connected? Are there common friends? Shared interests or organizations?

• Be clear and direct. Don't make the person being asked for help do any legwork. Be clear about what you are asking for or who you are looking to meet through this person. Remove all of the guesswork. If you are a jobseeker (the most common requests I receive are from this group), ask if you can forward your resume and target company list. This is very helpful.

WORST Practices for Seeking Help

• Don't be respectful of time and calendars. The person you are reaching out to may be extremely busy, and your need will likely not be their top priority. Acknowledge your respect for their calendar in your communication as you make your request.

• Act like you are old friends to people you barely know or don't know at all. A common complaint from other professionals is help requests from people they haven't seen in years, or have never met, who act like their best friend. It comes across as false and is an immediate turn-off.

• Make it all about you. Don't make your request about only your issues and needs. Inquire about the other person and how they are doing, and at least make it obvious you have some sincere interest.

• Use a shotgun approach. One of the most ineffective methods of asking for help is the blind copy approach where someone requests that we "keep them in mind if we see any interesting opportunities which fit their background." Another variation is to email someone directly with "I would love to meet anyone in your network who needs a good operations guy." This is ineffective and not likely to bring a positive result.

• Send an unsolicited request to connect on LinkedIn with minimal information. LinkedIn is a wonderful tool for building a network, but don't send random requests to connect without providing a reason. Positive examples: "We have several mutual friends" or "We worked together at ABC Company several years ago" or "I read an article in which you addressed connecting strategies. I have shared this with several friends and would like to connect with you, if you don't mind."

• Fail to follow up and show gratitude. This request for help should not be the only time you reach out to this individual. Follow up with the results of their assistance and absolutely let them know you are grateful.

We all need to ask for help, myself included. How we ask for this assistance is critical, and increasingly, it seems that many of us are forgetting the fundamentals of effective business communication. Nobody is discounting the genuine need for the active assistance of others in a job search, desire for new customers, need for advice, or whatever is behind the need to make these requests, but taking the time to gauge our approach and the potential response on the other end can make all the difference in making this effort more successful.

Power of Asking Questions
To Better Your Relationship with Your Wife

1. What are some things I do that make you feel special?

2. What are some things (both big and small) I do that irritate you?

3. What have been some specific times in our marriage when you have not felt like you were the most important aspect of my life?

4. What are sometimes you've felt the most loved by me? What specifically caused you to feel this way?

5. What are your greatest pain points as my wife and the kid's mom? What are the most difficult aspects of this dual role?

6. How can I better help with the kids day to day?

7. How can I better help around the house day to day?

9. What do you feel brings you the greatest joy in life?

10. What are some of the things we do that you find the most fun?

11. What does the ideal date night look like for you?

12. What does the ideal family day look like for you?

13. Do I draw you into too much of my job, or too little?

14. Do you feel that you have my full attention when I am home? If not,
what steals my attention? (i.e. phone, twitter, etc)

17. What is your greatest fear?

18. Are there things I can do to make your life easier in general?

19.   What's the biggest thing you would like to see change in our
       marriage/relationship?

Power of Asking Questions
to Better Your Relationship With Your Husband

Communication, or lack thereof, is the root of all problems in marriages. Instead of waiting for issues to arise and failing to communicate properly, sit down one night per week and ask your spouse these 10 questions (and don't forget to answer them yourself, too!).Instead of just settling for a 'good enough' marriage, let's work together to make it great. Ask anyone that's in a happy marriage how they do it — and "communication with each other" is bound to come up. If you have a hard time communicating with your partner, or even just want to take your marriage from great to outstanding, set aside some time each week to ask your husband these 10 questions.

These Power of Asking Questions will improve your marriage. So many times we get caught up in life - whether it is our business, the kids, errands- or we get so comfortable with the other person, we take them for granted and assume what they are thinking. We develop expectations which will breed resentments and break a marriage down quickly. If you are not married, this is still a good tool to help your relationship.

How was your week?
So simple, yet very rarely asked. Relationship expert Melissa Hargrove states that this is the most important question you can ask your spouse. "Without spelling out the question, it's very easy for your husband to feel taken for granted and even taken advantage of," she says.

What are your plans for the upcoming week?
Pull out the calendar and together discuss what each of you is doing for the week. Do you have a girls' night planned? Does he need to work late a few days? Fill each other in on your plans! Now is also the time to set aside a date night for the two of you. It doesn't have to be fancy — but schedule some downtime with each other midweek.

What can I do to help you this week?
Remember, marriage is a partnership. Sure, you may be swamped at work or busy running the kids around, but your marriage should be your first priority. Ask your husband what you can do this week to make his life a little easier. Chances are he'll be more than happy to lend a helping hand next time you ask, too.

Did I do anything to irritate you this past week?
Asking this question forces you to be vulnerable. Be careful not to be too
critical when answering the question, though. The goal is to work
through irritabilities with one another together. Maybe your husband
didn't call one night and came home late, leaving you unsure as to when
to make dinner. Maybe you took your bad day at work out on him and
spoiled the evening. Be open!

How can I make you feel loved?
In marriage, it's vital to feel loved by your spouse. This is different than
offering to help them. Maybe your husband feels loved when you pursue
him sexually, maybe he loves when you offer to make him his favorite
drink, or maybe he simply loves cuddling on the couch. If you don't ask
him though, you won't know.

Do you need some alone time this week?
Let's face it — we all need alone time. Husbands can sometimes feel
guilty for wanting alone time after work after you've been with the kids
all day. The truth is, he needs alone time just as much as you. Maybe
give him an hour on Tuesday after work, and he'll take the kids on
Wednesday evening for you. Remember, you're a team!

What made you the happiest this week?
The answer to this question may surprise you. You may have made your
husband's day when he came home to his favorite meal one night, or
maybe the best part of his week was watching his favorite TV show.
Whatever his answer, try to duplicate it this week!

Questions That Will Radically
Change Your Marriage

It is easy to go days, weeks, and even months without intentionally connecting with your spouse. You live in the same house, but stop sharing life together. It's gradual. It's incremental. It happens to the best of marriages/relationships.

1. How can I serve you this week?

You want to capture the heart of your spouse, so ask this question on Sunday night. It's easy to focus on our to-do list. We have plans; we have deadlines; we have obligations. But we open up a new level of intimacy in our marriage when we ask our spouse how we can place their needs ahead of our own.

2. What has you stressed or anxious?

Is there a question that communicates care and concern more than this question? When you ask this question, you are inviting your spouse to be vulnerable with you. You are also communicating to them, "You're not alone. I'm in this with you."

3. What is the most important thing you need to accomplish this week?

Unspoken expectations are always unmet expectations. Most of the conflict we experience in marriage derive from unmet expectations. If you know what your spouse needs to get done in a given week, you can be an ally for them in that process. For ex, I always appreciate when (Mike) asks me this question. It lets me know that he is interested in the details of my week.

5. What are we doing on our next date night?

If you don't plan a date night, then you probably won't have a date night. For us, Fridays are days we have off and our kids are in school. On Thursday, one of us will ask, "What do you want to do tomorrow?" It helps us be intentional about making one another a priority.

The truth is, it is a few small things that will make a HUGE difference. Take 30 minutes, ask your spouse these questions, and see if you don't see a few changes in your relationship this week.

Power of Asking Questions to Ask Your Boss

Think about it: You probably only hear from your boss when

a) You royally screwed up b) you did great work or c) it's performance review time.

Feedback from your supervisor is what you crave, unless you're happy flying under the radar, which certainly won't help you advance. Getting honest input from your supervisor is crucial to your relationship with your boss — and, like it or not, your relationship with your boss can make or break your career. A solid rapport makes deadlines a breeze, and the workday go by in a flash; but a shaky one can render even a short elevator ride uncomfortable.

Plus, having a good relationship with your boss may even reduce stress at work. In a workplace study by the American Psychological Association, up to 75 percent of respondents said the most stressful aspect of their job is their immediate boss.

Here, we asked an expert to share a few key questions you can ask that will help you and your supervisor get on (or stay on) the right track.

1. How was your weekend?

When to ask: It gives you an opportunity to start building a personal relationship and connect on a non-work level. Try to ask something specific, like if her daughter won her softball game or how the client dinner went — it'll show you've been paying attention.

Why it's important to ask: The more you know about your boss, the better. By understanding how she spends her time when she's not at the office, you'll learn what's important to her. "It allows you two to build a real relationship that extends beyond spreadsheets and timelines," Oprah says. "It gives you another dimension to connect on, so she also sees you as not just a subordinate, but someone with a personal life and outside interests, too. Furthermore, by sharing personal details about your life, you will appear more mature and invested in the relationship. That scores big points with management."

2. What's your biggest problem — and how can I help you solve it?

When to ask: This is a great query to bring up if you're new to a job or team because it will give you insight into the demands of the job. Another good time to ask this question is when a new supervisor joins your department; it will help you discover what his priorities are during the transition. But you can also use this question anytime; say, when you notice that your boss has a lot on her plate, and you want to let her know you're available to pitch in, which can boost your "invaluable employee" quotient.

Why it's important to ask: It shows that you're someone who is strategic and thoughtful and who takes initiative — you're not just waiting around to be told what to do.

3. When you think of the best employees who have worked for you, what makes them stand out in your mind?

When to ask: This isn't the type of question to pop as you head out to pick up a sandwich together. Reserve it for a time when you're in serious "getting feedback" mode, like during a performance review, or at a time when your boss has just given you a bit of tough feedback. This question can be a good way to signal that you want to improve and learn skills that will make her job easier — a task in any employee's job description.

Why it's important to ask: If you've got a good relationship with your boss, but you're looking to take your game to the next level or score a promotion or a raise, this is a great way to discover what she values most. Once you find out, you can try to model some of those behaviors.

4. I'm really excited about working on________together. Would it be possible to get some feedback from you over the course of the project?

When to ask: Anytime you start a new project, work with a new team, or work on a long-term assignment, let your manager know upfront that you'd like to sit down with him and get feedback from him once you're underway.

Why it's important to ask: Every time you ask your boss after an important meeting, "How'd that go?" invariably he'll say you did a great job. The best way to get real and meaningful input is to plant the seed in advance and ask your boss for feedback before you need it.

5. I really want to nail the_________assignment. Do you have any templates I could reference, or is there anyone on the team I should speak to who's done a good job on one recently?

When to ask: At the onset of a project that's unlike anything you've ever tackled.

Why it's important to ask: Most likely your boss has a vision of how she'd like a project completed, and if you don't have a clear sense of her expectations, she's bound to be disappointed. You don't need to reinvent the wheel when you get a new assignment. Be resourceful and ask to see examples of a job well done. By asking for guidance upfront, you're saving yourself — and your boss — from disappointment and lots of wasted time.

6. I'd love to oversee_________in the next six months. Could we keep that in mind as projects are being assigned?

When to ask: When you're excelling in your current role and ready for a new challenge — and you know your workload won't suffer for it.

Why it's important to ask: Managers love employees who are excited to learn, grow, and take on new responsibilities. When it comes time for promotion, you will fare well as someone who not only does a good job, but is always eager to develop new skills and add the most value to your organization.

7. What should I start doing? What should I stop doing? What should I continue doing that I do well?

When to ask: Ideally, these are questions that your boss will naturally answer during your performance review, but if not, you should feel free to ask. If you just had a review, and you don't feel that this information was offered, send your boss an email to request some one-on-one time and tell him that you're hoping to answer these specific questions.

Why it's important to ask: There are probably a lot of things you do well that your boss loves and probably others that he wishes you'd stop doing, but he never really had the heart or stomach to tell you. This line of questioning makes it easy for him to finally tell you that the 10 hours of cold-calling you're doing every week isn't leading to results, and you'd be better off building out the focus group strategy instead.

If your boss evades these questions — and says that you're doing a great job, and you don't need to change a thing, but you know there's room for improvement — you can gently press the issue. Try a follow-up question like, "I really appreciate hearing everything is going well, but I'd really like to move up a level and challenge myself. What else should I be doing to make sure I get promoted next year?"

8. I'm sure that I'll have some additional thoughts and questions as I digest all this information. Could we schedule a follow-up conversation in a few days?

When to ask: At the end of a not-so-great performance review or any conversation wherein your boss gives you valuable, if not altogether positive, feedback.

Why it's important to ask: It's hard to think on your feet and ask constructive questions when you're feeling beat up. By asking for a few days to collect your thoughts, you'll have time to reflect on your boss' words and brainstorm ways to move ahead. The last thing you want to do is lose your cool. Remember, the goal of feedback is not to make you feel good. It's to make you better at your job.

Power of Asking Questions to Ask Your Child

1. Tell me about the best part of your day.

2. What was the hardest thing you had to do today?

3. Did any of your classmates do anything funny?

4. Tell me about what you read in class.

5. Who did you play with today? What did you play?

6. Do you think math [or any subject] is too easy or too hard?

7. What's the biggest difference between this year and last year?

8. What rules are different at school than our rules at home? Do you think they're fair?

9. Who did you sit with at lunch?

10. Can you show me something you learned (or did) today?

Oprah's Power is The Power of Asking

Oprah was recently named by Forbes as #1 on the Celebrity 100 list. Her net worth is reported at $2.8 billion. Obviously, she's ambitious, resilient, and smart - so are a lot of other celebrities. But Oprah has a unique way of connecting with people (her guests and audience) that gets celebrities like Lance Armstrong to confess publicly. What does she do? She connects and influences others through the use of powerful questions.

The right questions inspire creativity, drive connection and engagement, and get better results. In my executive coaching practice, asking the right questions is the single most important tool I use to help others grow themselves as leaders. Here are ways to ask questions that work:

Inspire Creativity & Innovation

Statements can cause people to judge (agree or disagree) while questions help people tap into the part of the brain that is creative. Ask these questions:

- If we were to totally delight our customers what would that look and feel like to them?
- What does success look like in this situation?
- If resources were not constrained what could be possible here?

Sell Your Product or Idea

Questions help us better understand the needs of our customers:

- What are the most pressing issues or challenges you face?
- If we were to create the perfect solution for you, what would that look like?
- Why is this need area important to you?

Improve decision-making

Organizations are getting flatter hierarchies and wider span of controls. We can no longer afford to hold on to decision making authority or expect to be the expert in every situation. Tap into the expertise of those closest to the issues:

- What are your criteria for making this decision? Why?
- What options did you consider and reject?
- What assumptions have we made that we need to test?

Create a Learning Culture

The ability to take calculated risks and rapidly test and learn from failures is a key trait of learning organizations and successful leaders:

- What did we learn from this situation?
- What would we do differently in the future?
- How and where else can we apply this learning for greater success?

Direct Focus

Leaders have great power to direct the conversation in a way that builds a positive vision of what's possible:

- What's working well in this situation?
- What did we do to create that positive outcome?
- What could be a vision for this project that would really excite you to be part of it?

Engage and Influence

Working across organizational boundaries can sometimes feel like the battle lines are drawn as each area has unique goals. Questions help us influence others over whom we have no authority:

- What are your goals in this situation?
- What are some constraints you're facing and what would be possible if they were removed?
- How can I support you in that?

Develop Others

The Socratic Method is well-known for helping learning stick. Questions are critical in this process.

- What does success look like in this project to you?
- Which of your strengths will be critical to leverage?
- What support do you need from me?

Get Commitment to Change

The greatest challenge to any major change initiative is changing human behavior. How well does telling people what to do work? To capture commitment to change, ask:

- What are your objectives and goals? Why are they important to you?
- How can we make sure that this initiative helps you achieve your goals?
- What do you see as the enablers to implementation?

Motivate Ourselves

Are there times you wish you could better motivate yourself toward goals?

- Why is this goal really important to me? What's already working well?
- What have I done to create that success?
- What special talents or strengths do I have that can help me achieve my goals?

Grow in Our Own Self-Awareness

Self- awareness is critical to success. Ask yourself:

- What are strengths I have that can be leveraged at work?
- What brings me joy in the work that I do?

The Challenge

Asking questions can be difficult. It requires a shift in our own mindset.
We have to let go of three ego needs:

- The need to be superior or to prove ourselves (e.g.
  I'm the smartest person in the room, so let me tell
  you everything I know).
- The need to control outcomes (e.g. the best and most
  efficient way to do this is my way, so let me just help
  you by telling you what to do).
- The need for perfection without any tolerance for
  failure (e.g. we have to do this perfectly because
  anything less than success will make me look bad.)

The Final Act

The way you live is how you lead. The biggest question I am
asked daily is "how have you done it?" How have you done this
or that? My biggest secret has been that I asked, took action, and
did it whether I was afraid or not. Les Brown gets up on stage
and tells my story; after he finishes, people come up to me
amazed at everything I have accomplished. You read earlier
about my former husband having a brain injury, my cancer, my
father being terminally ill, and other challenges I have endured.
Guess what? My greatest accolades happened during this time. I
didn't allow the media, nay-sayers, and other people using the
excuse about a "down economy" to stop me. Remember, I am the
little girl who was told she would never amount to anything,
came from a family of alcoholics, but was surrounded by one
person who always believed in me, my dad.
Bottom line is this, you can do anything you put your mind to and
as Michael Beckwith stated on December 20, 2009, "Have courage
to believe what your mind thinks is impossible." I have, and so can
you, by using the power of asking.

The power of asking requires firm self-discipline. Remember the
mark of a real leader is the person who can create a plan for their
life and then follow it through, business or personal.

It will not be long before the skills you acquire from your
exercises begin to create positive results. Don't force it; calmly
imagine the end result. The more you work on your new
'thinking' self-image, the sooner you will develop a stellar self-
image that will be both unshaken by adversity and enable your
success; you will ask for what you want and deserve.

With practice, your image which began as a dream and grew into a
theory, will suddenly, magically become a fact and way of life!
Your upside-down thinking will affect and enhance your life
significantly.

And remember, when you are out there succeeding and living the
life you always dreamed of, it will be you who is becoming the role
model, the example of a true leader for future generations. "His
faithfulness is carried through all generations." Psalms 100:5

To Your Success and In Gratitude,

Bardi Toto

ABOUT THE AUTHOR

Bardi Toto is a NY Times Best Selling Author, loving mom of 2 grown boys, an everyday hero recognized on Values.com out of Millions of people for her Gratitude, Determination and Making a difference in the world on http://www.passiton.com/your-everyday-heroes. The foundation of her business and personal life is Gratitude. She shows Entrepreneurs and businesses HOW to implement Gratitude online. This includes their sales teams and business via social media.

Bardi has gotten world renowned recognition for The Power of Gratitude, amongst her other unique strategies which include Disrupt Your Brand. Her latest book Disrupt Your Brand featuring Gary Vaynerchuk is launching Mid-September 2025.

Bardi has been featured on The Daily Vee 478, featured in Entrepreneur Magazine, Forbes with her "Disruptive" Style of Branding and Marketing strategies implementing Gratitude. She has been featured on TV with her unique Branding/Marketing Strategies, books Disrupt Your Brand (2025) Kids for Gratitude for Parents and Educators, which include Fox, BOLD TV Business, Good Morning Texas, Living 808, ABC, CBS, NBC and The Morning Blend.

Bardi has also been on a variety of radio shows including IHeart radio where she has hosted several shows. Bardi has had 3 interviews with Gary Vaynerchuk and has interviewed Mike Ditka, TD Jakes, Real Talk Kim and many others of notoriety. She has also been in several business magazines which have strengthened her proven track record helping Authors, Small business owners, entrepreneurs, Fortune 500 companies and Professional businesses effectively use social media. Her book became a #1 Best Seller in LESS THAN 2 hrs. in the top 3 Categories.

Bardi has been named as a Global Goodwill Ambassador and received a humanitarian award representing the United States. Bardi is known for her Trademarked programs Disrupt Your Brand and The Invisible Branding Method, world renowned mentoring program, The Power of Asking amongst other programs.

Bardi has been interviewed several times by one of the Top Influencers on the internet Gary Vaynerchuk and featured as mentioned earlier on the Daily Vee.

Voted #2 out of the top 100 Branding Experts to follow on twitter and online. Founder and CEO of a Web Design, Branding/Digital Marketing Agency.

Her book The Power of Asking for Women "Creating All That You Want" is a gift from the heart. Bardi's goal is to change the lives of millions and make an impact in the world which she has already done with her attitude of gratitude and her heart.

Bardi Loves bringing others talents and gifts to the world with her unique Branding approach implementing gratitude that has been unseen online. She is internationally known for teaching How to Communicate on social media, building long term relationships and increasing business without selling.
She has implemented gratitude into her brand on social media and teaches others to do the same.

Bardi Shows people what to do hands on, rather than telling them what to do. Bardi will not tell you what you want to hear but what works and what doesn't. No Hype! With a strong background in the world of internet technology she has been working with various social networking giants like YouTube and Instagram,

She is passionate about showing fellow professionals how to develop powerful relationships using social media. Bardi provides her clients and students with a proven turnkey business model.

Bardi's Branding program is the best in the industry. It has helped many including Authors, Celebrities Speakers, entrepreneurs, musicians, corporations and small businesses catapult their success to the next level. She offers a unique mentoring program "Disrupt Your Brand" which helps you to achieve the success you were destined for.

Her new Power of Asking Mentorship program for Women is a unique blend of personalized coaching, branding and social media. Bardi also coaches' women worldwide on The Power of Asking, empowerment and leadership .

ONGOING ADVICE AS YOU IMPLEMENT THE POWER OF ASKING STRATEGIES

Living life and running a business - actually both can be hard. There are so many decisions to make. What if you had a mentor - a seasoned, experienced, personal and business professional supporting you, month after month, as you implement *The Power of Asking* strategies? On the business side, these are strategies which involve branding, social media, and negotiation. Bardi can assist you by putting your systems in place and manage your new- found revenue streams.

You can get this support when you join the...

The Power of Asking Coaching Program

Bardi will help you look at where you are now, then work with you to create a personalized plan for getting to where you want to be. Whether you're a business owner, an employee, or just considering starting a business of your own, she is there for you - advising you, providing accountability, working with your unique strengths and challenges, and moving you forward on your path.

Find out now how Bardi can help you:

Barditotocoaching.com – Book a Call

Instagram.com @barditoto

It starts with you and your happiness, ripples into the lives of others, and becomes a wave of positive change around the world. Pledge your voice to the Happiness Movement, share with others, and see how far your happiness can reach!

Barditotocoaching.com

Her Latest books are on Amazon, which include Disrupt
Your Brand, Kids for Gratitude for Parents and Educators,
The Power of Asking and Gratitude, Kids for Aloha and Transforming
Gratitude in the Workplace

Empower. Inspire. Transform.

Go to

barditotocoaching.com

instagram.com @ barditoto

RESOURCES

Resources & Hotlines for Help and Support

Suicide & Crisis Lifeline – 988
24/7, confidential support for anyone in emotional distress or suicidal crisis.

SAMHSA National Helpline – 1-800-662-HELP (4357)
24/7 treatment referral and information service for individuals facing mental
health or substance abuse challenges.

Crisis Text Line – Text HOME to 741741
Free, 24/7 confidential support via text message.

National Domestic Violence Hotline – 1-800-799-SAFE (7233)
24/7, confidential help for anyone experiencing domestic violence.

National Maternal Mental Health Hotline – 1-833-TLC-MAMA (852-6262)

Emotional support for pregnant and postpartum women, available 24/7.
211 Helpline (United Way) – 211

Free and confidential service that helps people across North America find local resources and support.

Joel Osteen Prayer Line – 1-888-567-JOEL (5635)
Billy Graham Prayer Line 24/7 – 1-855-255-PRAY

Her Latest books are on Amazon, which include Kids for Gratitude, The Power of Asking and Gratitude and Kids for Aloha

Empower. Inspire. Transform.

Go to

barditotocoaching.com